MANCHESTER UNITED
COLLECTIBLES

Iain McCartney

AMBERLEY

First published 2018

Amberley Publishing
The Hill, Stroud
Gloucestershire, GL5 4EP

www.amberley-books.com

Copyright © Iain McCartney, 2018

The right of Iain McCartney to be identified as
the Author of this work has been asserted in
accordance with the Copyrights, Designs and
Patents Act 1988.

ISBN 978 1 4456 8095 8 (print)
ISBN 978 1 4456 8096 5 (ebook)

British Library Cataloguing in Publication Data.
A catalogue record for this book is available from
the British Library.

Origination by Amberley Publishing.
Printed in the UK.

Contents

Introduction

There's More to United than just Watching!

For many, supporting Manchester United Football Club is nothing more than the enjoyment of watching the team in action on a match-by-match basis, be it at home or away. But for others their interest goes well beyond those ninety minutes through their interest in collecting memorabilia relating to the club and its players. Some are simply casual collectors, keeping their match tickets from those European away games or the *United Review* from their visits to Old Trafford, or other club programmes from trips to away grounds. But there are others for whom it is a serious hobby, collecting anything and everything that comes their way, or what their pocket can afford, and building up their own private, and totally personal, United Museum.

In the not too distant past, programmes – and to a lesser extent trade and cigarette cards – were the main, and arguably only collectables, with autographs bringing up the rear. Every football-loving schoolboy had them tucked away in drawers, cupboards and shoe boxes, but as the modern era arrived and those programme collections grew near completion, the collecting bug took them down new avenues to collect match tickets, badges, postcards, menus, newspapers and photographs, and in the modern era books, replica shirts and whatever else came their way, vying for a space in those ever-increasing collections.

Old players hitting hard times or looking to lay a firm financial footing for their families and content to simply have the memories began selling their prized medals, shirts and caps at specialist auctions, allowing those collectors with a bit of money in the bank, or an understanding partner, to purchase those unique, historical items that had been available in the past to only a handful of individuals.

Since 1990 I have been running the Manchester United Collectors Club, an organisation of like-minded United supporters that was established in 1981 by Alan Bradshaw, Kevin Burthem and Roy Cavanagh. Taking over the reins from Kevin, I produced six bi-monthly newsletters per year, covering every conceivable collectable thing on United. At times it was a struggle, but I have enjoyed every minute of getting to know many of the members, who are now also good friends and familiar faces at Old Trafford on match days.

I had toyed with putting together a book on United memorabilia in the past, but it never materialised, mainly due to writing other books on the club, many of which will be part of numerous collections in their own right. But when I was approached by Amberley at a time when I had more or less decided that my days as an author were coming to an end, I decided to sharpen the pencil, haul open the filing cabinet and cupboards and begin writing about the memorabilia I had accumulated since those first trade cards, and that first copy of the *United Review* ignited the flame.

There are better collections than mine, much better, but everyone's collection is unique within itself. Some might consider their collection as 'basic', and although it may lack the high value, unique bits and pieces, it is their own, painstakingly put together and something that they take pride in, adding to it if and when the occasion arises. Everyone to their own.

To compile a book such as this, and with the page and illustration restriction put on me by the publisher, there are numerous items that I might have wanted to include but am unable to simply due to space, so I have tried to cover as wide a cross section as I possibly can, while at the same time hoping to keep it as interesting as possible.

I must confess that when I started out I had no idea as to what would appear within the pages that follow. Yes there are programmes and the like that I knew beforehand would find a space within, but who knew what I would find tucked away in box files and cupboards that I would consider worth including?

Hopefully you will find the book enjoyable. If you already collect, then hopefully there is something here that you don't already have and can get added to your 'wants list'. If you are not yet a collector, or a serious one, then perhaps the book might inspire you to take your own collection a step further, or perhaps even start collecting different items relating to Manchester United Football Club.

There are still numerous programme dealers out there and the internet has opened countless new doors for the avid collector, with the more serious of the species being able to visit the memorabilia auctions that materialise on a regular basis.

Before bringing this introduction to a close and beginning the look through the various collectables, a word of warning for those of you setting out on the long and wonderful road of United collecting. Some United programmes have been reprinted, such as Red Star Belgrade away in 1957/58, the Sheffield Wednesday Cup Tie and Wolves No. 20 home issues from that same season – Anderlecht away, the first European Cup Tie in 1956, the 1909 Cup Final, George Best's debut against Burnley at Old Trafford in 1963, the very first match against Liverpool at Old Trafford among them – so be careful when you see them for sale.

Autographs can be another minefield, with numerous forgeries out there, more so in modern day signatures, which are rarely nothing more than a scribble with no real identifying twist of the pen. Forgeries also exist in the world of badges, or perhaps that should be better defined by saying old-style badges have been reproduced by modern dealers. So while you should enjoy the collecting of United memorabilia, also beware.

I also apologise for the sometimes continued reference to items being of historical interest, but any collection is something of a history of the Manchester United.

Iain McCartney, 2018

Chapter 1

From a Card to a Collection

I have had an interest in football for as long as I can remember, but how it progressed into something much more I do not know. My initial interest in Manchester United, however, does glimmer through the mists of time, as I can recall being at my grandmother's at a Saturday teatime and hearing a voice on the radio constantly mention the name of the club upon which I wouldn't develop simply a crush, but a full-blown love affair. Quite why the name 'Manchester United' became fixed in my tiny mind, I have no idea. It wasn't as if my grandmother knew much about football, nor did any of my other female relatives who were present at the time. My father didn't have a great interest in the game either. My uncle did, but did not cast any influence on my decision to affix myself to a team in red and white from so far away.

If anyone required proof of my long-lasting allegiance to a team from I knew not where – yes, I knew they were from Manchester, but had no idea where that was as I knew little of anything beyond the corner of south-west Scotland where I lived – then it is a Chix trade card album from the late 1950s into which I had pencilled the words 'Manchester United'. On looking at the album today, I notice that I actually misspelt the name of the street where I lived!

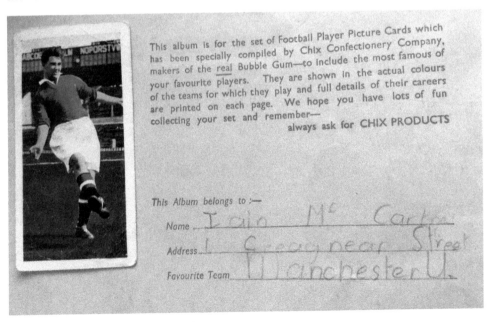

This album is for the set of Football Player Picture Cards which has been specially compiled by Chix Confectionery Company, makers of the real Bubble Gum—to include the most famous of your favourite players. They are shown in the actual colours of the teams for which they play and full details of their careers are printed on each page. We hope you have lots of fun collecting your set and remember—

always ask for CHIX PRODUCTS

This Album belongs to :—

Name ... Iain Mc Carter

Address ... 1 Craig near Street. Manchester

Favourite Team ... Manchester U.

Chix card album/Jackie Blanchflower card.

Of the cards featuring United players in that particular series, that of Jackie Blanchflower, for some unknown reason, was my favourite. Why the album and cards have survived after so long is another of life's mysteries.

So, my collection of Manchester United memorabilia had unknowingly been launched with the above card and also those of Jackie's teammates, Roger Byrne, Duncan Edwards and the more unfamiliar Jeff Whitefoot, in that same Chix set.

But it wasn't just Manchester United – I just couldn't get enough football, and countless sets of cards were collected in the months and years ahead. *Football Monthly* began to fall through the letter box on a regular basis and Christmas was eagerly looked forward to with the appearance of numerous annuals I had requested from good old Santa Claus.

Out of the blue, programmes made an appearance on the scene (the first possibly being a Queen of the South *v.* Millwall friendly) and soon became not simply a collectable item, but an obsession, the staple diet. I wanted as many as I could get and, like many others, sent off for bundles of them as advertised in *Football Monthly*. That magazine, as did its less lavish, but equally enjoyable stablemate *Soccer Star*, also carried excellent adverts for selling and exchanging programmes with fellow enthusiasts; another memory of a bygone age.

Although I had a small handful of programmes, the United collection had still not increased beyond the colourful trade cards, so a United programme became a 'must have'. So, off to Old Trafford I wrote, requesting one from a recent game. A short while later that first *United Review* duly appeared, folded and with the word 'note' written below the 6*d* price. I had only sent 3*d* with the stamped addressed envelope, but I think I have more than paid the outstanding balance over the intervening years! The programme remains in the collection, imperfect with folds and the writing on the front, but I never felt like replacing it as this was a unique item, and the first of many.

The mid-1960s saw those 'other' programmes discarded along the way, some to my regret now, but those bundles of various club and international programmes were to be replaced by similar bundles of United home programmes; not just ordinary league games, but also those seemingly exotic European ties. The collection was increasing slowly, now gaining momentum with a handful of cards and some programmes, similar to many other football-mad boys of the time. I was completely unaware, however, that it was not simply a passing fad, and little did I know what was to be accumulated in the years ahead.

Even my mother was to become involuntarily involved, as she was suddenly forced into forsaking her usually preferred brand of tea and persuaded to buy Typhoo as they began issuing photographs of players and teams on the side of their packets in 1963–64, which continued sporadically until the early 1970s.

Not only were the black and white photographs on the packets collectable in their own right, but if you collected a dozen and sent them back to Typhoo you would receive in exchange a large colour team group of your choice, or later that of an individual player. Both were of excellent quality and highly collectable even today.

As the months and years passed by the cards were to become secondary and I was soon concentrating on building a United programme collection. Gone was the schoolboy shoebox containing a mixture of club and international programmes; it was suddenly just all about United. Every issue, home and away, back to the 1946/47 season was in my sights, although I had no idea at that time as to the near impossibility of the completion of such a collection, from either an obtainable or a financial point of view.

Left: United *v.* Burnley programme, 1962/63.

Below: Typhoo team card.

MANCHESTER UNITED F.C.

Back row, L to R: Brennan, Stiles, Dunne (T.), Dunne (P.), Foulkes, Crerand
Front row, L to R: Connelly, Herd, Law, Charlton, Best

Chapter 2

Programmes and the Holy Grail

Unless you have a thick wallet, coupled with considerable luck, completing a collection of post-war United programmes is nigh on impossible. Firstly, you are in competition with countless others, and secondly, many are chasing the same late 1940s and early 1950s away issues, mainly against the likes of North East clubs Sunderland and Middlesbrough. But fear not, you can still assemble a good collection, and certainly an interesting one from a historical point of view, without a huge outlay or encountering too many problems.

If you are yet to venture down the road of programme collecting from the post-war period and your budget is tight, then you could do worse than to simply collect issues of historical interest such as Cup Finals, or expand that to a complete cup run, a certain player's debut, a significant victory; the choice is varied and yours alone.

Grimsby, 1946/47.

You could kick off with the first game after the Second World War, against Grimsby Town on 31 August 1946, the game played at Manchester City's Maine Road ground due to Old Trafford having been considerably damaged by German bombs. This is the very first *United Review* with its familiar, and much loved, player and supporter shaking hands. The first actual 'home' programme was not to appear until 24 August 1949 against Bolton Wanderers, when the cover showed a photograph of Old Trafford following the restoration work that had been painstakingly carried out following the war. Note in the photograph the roofless main stand.

With a post-war history second to none, there is a huge choice when it comes to collecting United programmes in a non-serious manner; by that I mean not attempting to obtain every single issue. So, from a historical point of view, there a few worth seeking out, such as the 1948 FA Cup Final against Blackpool, that first post-war trophy success, as well as another fixture against Blackpool some twenty-seven years later, when a packed Old Trafford saw the presentation of the Second Division championship trophy.

Then of course there are the European programmes, which is another avenue you could choose to go down. Again there are pitfalls, as that first away issue against Anderlecht in the 1956/57 season is very difficult to obtain. Borussia Dortmund from that same season, however, is just the opposite. Should you want a programme from

Above left: Blackpool FACF, 1948.

Above right: Blackpool, 1974/75.

Above left: Dortmund away, 1956.

Above right: Northampton away, 1969/70.

Right: Hibs away, 1948.

a truly memorable game (other than that 1999 Champions League Final) what about Northampton Town away in the 1969/70 season, when George Best scored 6 goals in an 8-2 win?

Post-war friendlies can widen the collection to a greater number of clubs, both in the United Kingdom and overseas, but again the expense factor comes into play with those early American tour issues not simply being rare, but expensive. One of the easier issues to find, and a particular favourite, is from a match against Hibs at Easter Road, Edinburgh, which was a benefit match for the late William McCartney in September 1948.

I can still remember getting this programme through the post. I am not entirely sure where it came from, but there is a good chance that it was from Sports Programmes. This was a programme I really wanted as William McCartney was my grandfather's cousin and his father John had actually played for and captained Newton Heath back in the 1890s.

The 1957/58 season in itself is well worth collecting and one that conjures up four very collectable programmes; or perhaps that should read three, as one is nigh impossible to obtain. These are not just great additions to the archives, but poignant memories of those 'Busby Babes'.

The first is that last match on English soil against Arsenal at Highbury on 1 February 1958, followed by the European tie the following Wednesday in Belgrade against Red Star. The latter I first saw for sale on a list from Sports Programmes in the 1970s.

Above left: Arsenal away, 1957/58.

Above right: Red Star away, 1957/58.

MANCHESTER UNITED v IPSWICH TOWN

After a week of the heaviest snowfall Old Trafford took on an Alpine look for the 4th Round Cup Tie versus Ipswich. Here a shot from Viollet (extreme right) tests Ipswich goalkeeper Bailey whilst Malcolm runs in from the left. Scanlon is poised to the rear. The shot missed but two others didn't making the score 2-0.   *Photo by courtesy of the Daily Mail*

Wolves postpones, 1957/8.

No 'offers invited for' back then, it was simply either write off or telephone in the hope that a particular item was still available. The Red Star issue was up for grabs at £10, but you have to remember that £10 was a considerable amount back then and a price I considered more than I wanted to pay.

It was to remain at the top of the 'wants list' for some time, but it seldom appeared for sale, until one day a dealer friend got in touch to say he had a copy in mint condition. An exchange was set up and agreed and I finally got my hands on it one match day. I have to add that those programmes I exchanged would fetch much more than that Belgrade issue. But that was then; today it usually sells for between £1,500 and £2,000.

Had the disaster at Munich not occurred, then United were scheduled to face Wolves at Old Trafford in a top of the table clash on 8 February. For obvious reasons the match was postponed, but the printing of the *United Review* for the fixture was underway, although it was brought to a halt when news of the disaster filtered through. The copies of the programme that had already been printed were then destroyed, although one or two were kept as poignant souvenirs by those working there. A few copies of this No. 20 *Review* still survive today, but attract bids of well into four figures when they go up for auction.

The fourth of the quartet of collectable issues from the 1957/58 season is another *United Review* that is far more common than the previously mentioned Wolves issue and one that will be filed away in almost all United collections – Sheffield Wednesday

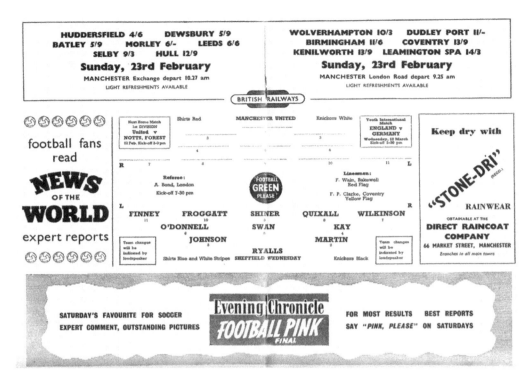

Sheffield Wednesday FAC, 1957/58.

in the FA Cup, the first game after the crash on 19 February. Although I say this is a common programme, some may find what could be classed a mint condition issue hard to come by as the United team in the centre pages was nothing more than eleven blank spaces since no one, not even caretaker manager Jimmy Murphy, knew what the line-up would be when the programme went to print. Many who attended on the night, and some collectors later on, filled in the names of the players who took the field that night, but most want a copy of the blank team sheet. Some have added both to the collection, while also seeking out a copy with the much-beloved programme token intact.

For those unaware as regards the 'token', this was a numbered square that was included on a page within each first team programme and on the single sheet reserve issues from 1956. When a big game came around the club would ask supporters for a certain number of tokens, which were affixed to the token sheet that was included in one of the early season programmes. This progressed into the 1990s, when the club then asked for the centre of the match ticket as proof you had attended games. Some collectors will only collect programmes with the token intact. Adding something of a postscript, United did issue programmes with a blank space where the token should be. Those were generally sent to people who wrote to the club asking for a particular issue.

I could fill the whole book with collectable programmes, and from the years following Munich there are many, but as mentioned before, if you are setting out on the collecting road, or are indeed thinking about trimming the collection, then purchase, or keep, those of historical interest.

UNITED REVIEW

MANCHESTER
UNITED
FOOTBALL CLUB

F.A. YOUTH CUP
FINAL 1st Leg
UNITED
v.
WOLVES
Kick-off 6-45 p.m.

1953-54
SEASON

23rd APRIL

2d.

SPECIAL ISSUE

OFFICIAL   PROGRAMME

F.A. YOUTH CHALLENGE CUP

Full details of this season's Competition are given on the inside pages.

Photo by C. F. Andrews of Stretford

FA Youth Cup issue.

Left: Trial match programme from 1954.

Below: Issue from The Cliff.

Floodlit Football Match at The Cliff, Broughton

FRIENDLY MATCH

Manchester United XI v. Northern Nomads
WEDNESDAY, 3rd DECEMBER, 1952   **Kick Off 7-15 p.m.**

MANCHESTER UNITED XI
RED SHIRTS AND WHITE SHORTS

CLAYTON

FULTON   KENNEDY

CAREY   JONES   EDWARDS

HAMPSON   McFARLANE   MOONEY   DOHERTY   ROWLEY

Referee: S. WOODWARD   Linesmen: J. S. ORCHARD, R. HARDING

GOALEN   BROMILOW   FAIRCLOUGH   WALTON   BIGLEY

WADE   LANGFORD   MURRAY

BOOTH   CHILDS

SHERRIFF

NORTHERN NOMADS
AMBER SHIRTS AND WHITE SHORTS

TO READ—HOLD PROGRAMME TO LIGHT   ★   Price 1d.

Also very collectable are the programmes from FA Youth Cup ties, especially the initial five seasons of the competition when United ruled the roost, and from the pre-season trial games that were played prior to the start of each season up until the early 1960s, when all four teams – first, reserves, 'A' and 'B' – would play each other on the same afternoon.

Even more collectable are the difficult to obtain single sheet issues from games played at The Cliff training ground in those immediate post-war years. 'To Read – Hold Programme To Light' was the legend along the bottom of those flimsy issues.

Wartime issues were also, for United home fixtures at least, little more than single sheets, which have done well to survive the tests of time.

What about pre-war programmes or Newton Heath issues, I hear you ask? Yes, they are out there, the latter only appearing every so often, but almost every auction of football memorabilia has the odd few of the former up for grabs, but priced at well into three figures – higher than those of any other club.

In those pre-war years United changed the cover images a few times, so it is perhaps worth trying to obtain a copy of each, similar to the ones shown alongside. One question mark does arise as regards to the 1928 issue, which carried the masthead 'Red & White' while being printed in blue!

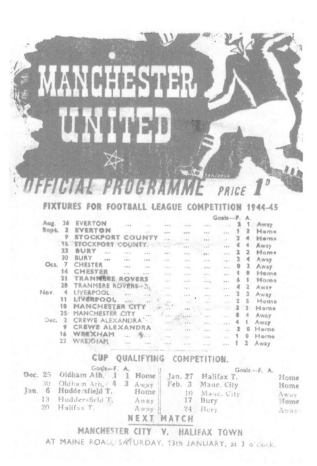

War-time issue.

VOL. XV. No. 34.   WEDNESDAY, MARCH 14, 1928.   2D.

FIXTURES and RESULTS, 1927-8.

LEAGUE—Division I.			CENTRAL LEAGUE.		
Aug.	27—MIDDLESBROUGH	Home..3-0	Aug. 27—BIRMINGHAM	Away..4-1	
	29—THE WEDNESDAY	Away..2-0	Sept. 3—STOKE CITY	Home..3-0	
Sept.	3—BIRMINGHAM	Away..0-0		10—WEST BROMWICH ALBION	Away..0-3
	7—THE WEDNESDAY	Home..1-1		12—THE WEDNESDAY	Away..3-4
	10—NEWCASTLE UNITED	Home..1-7		17—HUDDERSFIELD TOWN	Home..1-0
	17—HUDDERSFIELD TOWN	Away..2-4		28—THE WEDNESDAY	Home..3-2
	19—BLACKBURN ROVERS	Away..0-3	Oct. 1—MANCHESTER CITY	Home..0-2	
	24—TOTTENHAM HOTSPUR	Home..3-0		8—EVERTON	Home..2-1
Oct.	1—LEICESTER CITY	Away..0-1		15—BLACKPOOL	Away..0-3
	8—EVERTON	Away..2-5		19—LIVERPOOL	Away..2-2
	15—CARDIFF CITY	Home..2-2		29—PRESTON NORTH END	Home..3-0
	22—DERBY COUNTY	Home..5-0	Nov. 5—BURNLEY	Away..6-1	
	29—WEST HAM UNITED	Away..2-1		12—BURY	Home..1-1
Nov.	5—PORTSMOUTH	Home..2-0		19—SHEFFIELD UNITED	Away..0-2
	12—SUNDERLAND	Away..1-4		26—ASTON VILLA	Home..5-1
	19—ASTON VILLA	Home..5-1	Dec. 3—WOLVERHAMPTON WANDERERS..Away..1-0		
	26—BURNLEY	Away..0-4		10—DERBY COUNTY	Home..1-1
Dec.	3—BURY	Home..0-1		17—LEEDS UNITED	Away..1-3
	10—SHEFFIELD UNITED	Away..1-2		24—BRADFORD CITY	Home..4-1
	17—ARSENAL	Home..4-1		26—BLACKBURN ROVERS	Away..2-8
	24—LIVERPOOL	Away..0-2		31—BIRMINGHAM	Home..5-1
	26—BLACKBURN ROVERS	Home..1-1	**1928**		
	31—MIDDLESBROUGH	Away..2-1	Jan. 2—BLACKBURN ROVERS	Home..4-1	
1928				7—STOKE CITY	Away..0-3
Jan.	7—BIRMINGHAM	Home..1-1		14—OLDHAM ATHLETIC	Away..0-2
	14—BRENTFORD (F.A.C. 3rd Rd.)..Home..7-1			21—WEST BROMWICH ALBION	Home..5-2
	21—NEWCASTLE UNITED	Away..1-4		28—SHEFFIELD UNITED	Home..2-2
	28—BURY (F.A.C. 4th Rd.)	Away..1-1	Feb. 1—HUDDERSFIELD TOWN	Away..0-4	
Feb.	1—BURY (F.A.C. 4th Rd. Replay)..Home..1-0			4—OLDHAM ATHLETIC	Home..7-0
	4—TOTTENHAM HOTSPUR	Away..1-4		11—MANCHESTER CITY	Away..3-1
	11—LEICESTER CITY	Home..5-2		18—EVERTON	Away..3-2
	18—BIRMINGHAM (F.A.C. 5th Rd.)..Home..1-0			25—BLACKPOOL	Home..3-1
	25—CARDIFF CITY	Away..0-2	Mar. 3—LIVERPOOL	Home..0-0	
Mar.	3—BLACKBURN R. (F.A.C. 6th Rd.)..Away..0-2			10—PRESTON NORTH END	Away..2-2
	7—HUDDERSFIELD TOWN	Home..0-0		17—BURNLEY	Home..
	10—WEST HAM UNITED	Home..1-1		24—BURY	Away..
	14—EVERTON	Home..	April 7—BOLTON WANDERERS	Home..	
	17—PORTSMOUTH	Away..		7—ASTON VILLA	Away..
	24—H'FIELD T v S'FIELD U (F.A.S.F)Home..			9—BOLTON WANDERERS	Away..
	31—ASTON VILLA	Away..		14—WOLVERHAMPTON WANDERERS..Home..
April	6—BOLTON WANDERERS	Away..		21—DERBY COUNTY	Away..
	7—BURNLEY	Home..		28—LEEDS UNITED	Home..
	9—BOLTON WANDERERS	Home..	May 5—BRADFORD CITY	Away..	
	14—BURY	Away..			
	21—SHEFFIELD UNITED	Home..			
	28—ARSENAL	Away..			
May	—LIVERPOOL	Home..			
	—DERBY COUNTY	Away..			
	—SUNDERLAND	Home..			

ALLIED NEWSPAPERS LIMITED, Printers, Withy Grove, Manchester.

Pre-war issue.

LEAGUE CHAMPIONS, 1908-11. **RED & WHITE** **WINNERS ENGLISH CUP, 1909.**

MANCHESTER UNITED OFFICIAL PROGRAMME
SEASON 1928-29.

VOL. XVI.   No. 2.   WEDNESDAY, AUGUST 29, 1928.   **1D.**

FIXTURES and RESULTS, 1928-9.

. ∘ ○ ∘ .

LEAGUE—Division I.

Aug.	25—LEICESTER CITY	Home	1-1
,,	27—ASTON VILLA	Away	0-0
Sept.	1—MANCHESTER CITY	Away	
,,	8—LEEDS UNITED	Away	
,,	15—LIVERPOOL	Home	
,,	22—WEST HAM UNITED	Away	
,,	29—NEWCASTLE UNITED	Home	
Oct.	6—BURNLEY	Away	
,,	13—CARDIFF CITY	Home	
,,	20—BIRMINGHAM	Home	
,,	27—HUDDERSFIELD TOWN	Away	
Nov.	3—BOLTON WANDERERS	Home	
,,	10—SHEFFIELD WEDNESDAY	Away	
,,	17—DERBY COUNTY	Home	
,,	24—SUNDERLAND	Away	
Dec.	1—BLACKBURN ROVERS	Away	
,,	8—ARSENAL	Away	
,,	15—EVERTON	Home	
,,	22—PORTSMOUTH	Away	
,,	25—SHEFFIELD UNITED	Home	
,,	26—SHEFFIELD UNITED	Away	
,,	29—LEICESTER CITY	Away	
1929			
Jan.	1—ASTON VILLA	Home	
,,	5—MANCHESTER CITY	Home	
,,	12—(E.C. 3rd Round)		
,,	19—LEEDS UNITED	Home	
,,	26—LIVERPOOL (E.C., 4th Round)	Away	
Feb.	2—WEST HAM UNITED	Home	
,,	9—NEWCASTLE UNITED	Away	
,,	16—BURNLEY (E.C., 5th Round)	Home	
,,	23—CARDIFF CITY	Away	
Mar.	2—BIRMINGHAM (E.C., 6th Round)	Away	
,,	9—HUDDERSFIELD TOWN	Home	
,,	16—BOLTON WANDERERS	Away	
,,	23—SHEFFIELD WED.(E.C., Semi-final)	Home	
,,	29—BURY	Away	
,,	30—DERBY COUNTY	Away	
April	1—BURY	Home	
,,	6—SUNDERLAND	Home	
,,	13—BLACKBURN ROVERS	Away	
,,	20—ARSENAL	Home	
,,	27—EVERTON (E.C., Final)	Away	
May	4—PORTSMOUTH	Home	

CENTRAL LEAGUE.

Aug.	25—ASTON VILLA	Away	3-6
,,	29—MANCHESTER CITY	Home	
Sept.	3—WOLVERHAMPTON WANDERERS	Away	
,,	8—STOCKPORT COUNTY	Home	
,,	15—LEEDS UNITED	Away	
,,	17—STOCKPORT COUNTY	Away	
,,	22—LIVERPOOL	Home	
,,	26—MANCHESTER CITY	Away	
,,	29—BURNLEY	Away	
Oct.	6—PRESTON NORTH END	Home	
,,	13—SHEFFIELD UNITED	Away	
,,	20—STOKE CITY	Away	
,,	27—HUDDERSFIELD TOWN	Home	
Nov.	3—EVERTON	Away	
,,	10—BLACKBURN ROVERS	Home	
,,	17—BLACKPOOL	Away	
,,	24—DERBY COUNTY	Home	
Dec.	1—SHEFFIELD WEDNESDAY	Away	
,,	8—BOLTON WANDERERS	Home	
,,	15—BIRMINGHAM	Away	
,,	22—WEST BROMWICH ALBION	Home	
,,	25—OLDHAM ATHLETIC	Away	
,,	26—OLDHAM ATHLETIC	Home	
,,	29—ASTON VILLA	Home	
1929			
Jan.	12—WOLVERHAMPTON WANDERERS	Home	
,,	26—LEEDS UNITED	Home	
Feb.	2—LIVERPOOL	Away	
,,	9—BURNLEY	Home	
,,	16—PRESTON NORTH END	Away	
,,	23—SHEFFIELD UNITED	Home	
Mar.	2—STOKE CITY	Home	
,,	9—HUDDERSFIELD TOWN	Away	
,,	16—EVERTON	Home	
,,	23—BLACKBURN ROVERS	Away	
,,	29—BURY	Home	
,,	30—BLACKPOOL	Home	
April	1—BURY	Away	
,,	6—DERBY COUNTY	Away	
,,	13—SHEFFIELD WEDNESDAY	Home	
,,	20—BOLTON WANDERERS	Home	
,,	27—BIRMINGHAM	Home	
May	4—WEST BROMWICH ALBION	Away	

ALLIED NEWSPAPERS LIMITED, Printers, Withy Grove, Manchester.

Pre-war issue.

League Champions 1908-11

English Cup Winners 1909

MANCHESTER UNITED

OFFICIAL PROGRAMME & GUIDE

SEASON 1931–32.

VOL. XIX. No. 13.   SATURDAY, OCT. 31st, 1931.   1ᴰ.

FIXTURES AND RESULTS, 1931-32

FIRST LEAGUE TEAM.

1931.
Aug.	29—Bradford	Away	1—3
Sept.	2—Southampton	Home	2—3
,,	5—Swansea Town	Home	2—1
,,	7—Stoke City	Away	0—3
,,	12—Tottenham Hotspur	Home	1—1
,,	16—Stoke City	Home	1—1
,,	19—Nottingham Forest	Away	1—2
,,	26—Chesterfield	Home	3—1
Oct.	3—Burnley	Away	0—2
,,	10—Preston North End	Home	3—2
,,	17—Barnsley	Away	0—0
,,	24—Notts County	Home	3—3
,,	31—Plymouth Argyle	Away	
Nov.	7—Leeds United	Home	
,,	14—Oldham Athletic	Away	
,,	21—Bury	Home	
,,	28—Port Vale	Away	
Dec.	5—Millwall	Home	
,,	12—Bradford City	Away	
,,	19—Bristol City	Home	
,,	25—Wolverhampton W.	Home	
,,	26—Wolverhampton W.	Away	

1932.
Jan.	2—Bradford	Home	
,,	9—E.C. Third Round		
,,	16—Swansea Town	Away	
,,	23—Tottenham H. (E.C.4)	Away	
,,	30—Nottingham Forest	Home	
Feb.	6—Chesterfield	Away	
,,	13—Burnley (E.C.5)	Home	
,,	20—Preston North End	Away	
,,	27—Barnsley (E.C.6)	Home	
Mar.	5—Notts County	Away	
,,	12—Plymouth Argyle (S.F.)	Home	
,,	19—Leeds United	Away	
,,	25—Charlton Athletic	Home	
,,	26—Oldham Athletic	Home	
,,	28—Charlton Ath.	Away	
April	2—Bury	Away	
,,	9—Port Vale	Home	
,,	16—Millwall	Away	
,,	23—Bradford City (E.C.F.)	Home	
,,	30—Bristol City	Home	
May	7—Southampton	Away	

CENTRAL LEAGUE TEAM.

1931.
Aug.	29—Aston Villa	Home	1—2
Sept.	2—Bolton Wanderers	Away	0—5
,,	5—Manchester City	Away	3—4
,,	9—Huddersfield Town	Home	3—0
,,	12—Liverpool	Away	0—2
,,	14—Huddersfield Town	Away	0—1
,,	19—Stockport County	Home	1—1
,,	26—Preston North End	Away	3—2
,,	28—Stoke City	Away	1—2
Oct.	3—Sheffield Wed.	Home	5—0
,,	10—Burnley	Away	1—2
,,	17—Birmingham	Home	1—2
,,	24—Leeds United	Away	0—5
,,	31—West Bromwich A.	Home	
Nov.	7—Derby County	Away	
,,	14—Bury	Home	
,,	21—Blackburn Rovers	Away	
,,	28—Sheffield United	Home	
Dec	5—Blackpool	Away	
,,	12—Oldham Athletic	Home	
,,	19—Everton	Away	
,,	25—Wolverhampton W.	Away	
,,	26—Wolverhampton W.	Home	

1932.
Jan.	2—Aston Villa	Away	
,,	9—		
,,	16—Manchester City	Home	
,,	23—Liverpool	Home	
,,	30—Stockport County	Away	
Feb.	6—Preston North End	Home	
,,	13—Sheffield Wed.	Away	
,,	20—Burnley	Home	
,,	27—Birmingham	Away	
Mar.	5—Leeds United	Home	
,,	12—West Bromwich A.	Away	
,,	19—Derby County	Home	
,,	26—Bury	Away	
,,	28—Stoke City	Home	
April	2—Blackburn Rovers	Home	
,,	9—Sheffield United	Away	
,,	16—Blackpool	Home	
,,	23—Oldham Athletic	Away	
,,	30—Everton	Home	
May	7—Bolton Wanderers	Home	

J. W. Jarvis, Printer, 170 Stockport Road, Levenshulme.

Pre-war issue.

Pre-war issue.

Most programmes today are of course little more than miniature magazines, although some clubs do try and stick with the traditional, or at least indulge in a little nostalgia. Overpriced, too bulky to store and too little reading are three of the reasons many have now forsaken collecting them, instead simply trying to obtain a team sheet for the game.

In the past these team sheets were only available to the press and in the director's box, but today, with countless hospitality areas in stadiums, they have become readily available. They are perhaps a much better item to collect as they give you the exact line-ups for the game and not simply a long list of players and their squad numbers.

Without doubt my favourite team sheet comes from the 1999 Champions League Final, as it is the after match one that UEFA used to produce – not sure if they still do or not. This not only gave the two line-ups, but all the match details, which is something no programme could ever offer.

Before drifting away from programmes, it is worth remembering that there are another two types out there: pirate and postponed. For the uninitiated, the latter requires no explanation, so it is simply a case of stating that as far as I am aware there is a programme for every United match that has been postponed. This is due to the fact that most, if not all, were postponed on either the day of the actual match or the

Full Time Report
26 May 1999 Barcelona Final

MANCHESTER UNITED FC	FC BAYERN MÜNCHEN

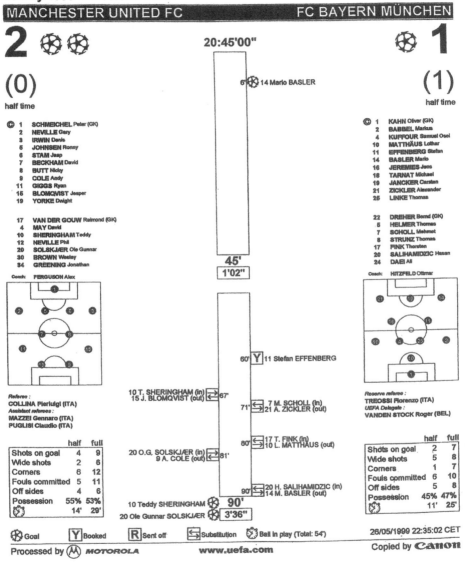

2 🏐🏐   20:45'00"   🏐 **1**

(0)   6' 🏐 14 Mario BASLER   **(1)**

half time   half time

	Manchester United		Bayern München
© 1	SCHMEICHEL Peter (GK)	© 1	KAHN Oliver (GK)
2	NEVILLE Gary	2	BABBEL Markus
3	IRWIN Denis	4	KUFFOUR Samuel Osei
5	JOHNSEN Ronny	10	MATTHÄUS Lothar
6	STAM Jaap	11	EFFENBERG Stefan
7	BECKHAM David	14	BASLER Mario
8	BUTT Nicky	16	JEREMIES Jens
9	COLE Andy	18	TARNAT Michael
11	GIGGS Ryan	19	JANCKER Carsten
15	BLOMQVIST Jesper	21	ZICKLER Alexander
19	YORKE Dwight	25	LINKE Thomas

17	VAN DER GOUW Raimond (GK)	22	DREHER Bernd (GK)
4	MAY David	5	HELMER Thomas
10	SHERINGHAM Teddy	7	SCHOLL Mehmet
12	NEVILLE Phil	8	STRUNZ Thomas
20	SOLSKJÆR Ole Gunnar	17	FINK Thorsten
30	BROWN Wesley	20	SALIHAMIDZIC Hasan
34	GREENING Jonathan	24	DAEI Ali

Coach: FERGUSON Alex   Coach: HITZFELD Ottmar

45'
1'02"

Referee :
COLLINA Pierluigi (ITA)
Assistant referees :
MAZZEI Gennaro (ITA)
PUGLISI Claudio (ITA)

Reserve referee :
TREOSSI Florenzo (ITA)
UEFA Delegate :
VANDEN STOCK Roger (BEL)

60' Y 11 Stefan EFFENBERG

10 T. SHERINGHAM (in) → 67'
15 J. BLOMQVIST (out)

71' ← 7 M. SCHOLL (in)
21 A. ZICKLER (out)

80' ← 17 T. FINK (in)
10 L. MATTHÄUS (out)

20 O.G. SOLSKJÆR (in) → 81'
9 A. COLE (out)

90' ← 20 H. SALIHAMIDZIC (in)
14 M. BASLER (out)

10 Teddy SHERINGHAM 🏐 **90'**
20 Ole Gunnar SOLSKJÆR 🏐 **3'36"**

	half	full		half	full
Shots on goal	4	9	Shots on goal	2	7
Wide shots	2	6	Wide shots	5	8
Corners	6	12	Corners	1	7
Fouls committed	5	11	Fouls committed	6	10
Off sides	4	6	Off sides	5	8
Possession	55%	53%	Possession	45%	47%
🏐	14'	29'	🏐	11'	25'

🏐 Goal	Y Booked	R Sent off	⇄ Substitution	🏐 Ball in play (Total: 54')

26/05/1999 22:35:02 CET

Processed by (M) **MOTOROLA**   **www.uefa.com**   Copied by **Canon**

1999 Champions League Final team sheet.

day before, when the programme had already been printed. Some are easy to find, but are perhaps not cheap. Others, like the previously mentioned Wolves issue from 1958, are ultra-rare.

As for pirate issues, these come mainly from the 1940s, '50s and '60s, usually originating from London. They consist normally of four pages on thicker than normal paper with only the team line-ups and match details having anything to do with the fixture as the photographic content on the cover and back pages were often of players who had nothing at all to do with the match.

Poorly produced – or perhaps it would be better to say that they were a complete waste of money on the day – with many supporters duped into parting with their hard-earned cash for what they thought was the actual match programme, they are, however, collectable in their own right today.

Real Madrid pirate
programme.

Chapter 3

Autographs, Badges and Tickets

With the Red Star issue safely tucked away, the wants list was down to a mere half dozen or so, all away issues from the late 1940s and early 1950s, but not including those from the numerous postponed games, of which there were quite a few. As all the serious United collectors were unfortunately after the same ones prices began to soar, so it was time to move in a different direction. It was now that the United collection gave a new meaning to the lyrics from one of my favourite groups, The Temptations, and their Motown track 'It's Growing': 'Like a snowball rolling down the side of a snow covered hill (it's growing). Like the size of the fish that he man claims broke his reel (it's growing)...' And grow it certainly did.

Apart from the likes of United photographs and articles in the popular magazines *Football Monthly* and *Soccer Star*, the first non-programme United item I got was a signed photograph of George Best. I had written to George c/o Old Trafford simply asking for his autograph and was pleasantly surprised to receive the signed black and white photograph. Strangely, I have never seen another similar to it.

Another early branch of the collecting tree was badges. Again I wrote off for a United Supporters Club badge and back one came, and this particular collection area was added to upon my first visit to Old Trafford when I bought small tin badges in the United Souvenir Shop of the players who had recently won the European Cup. I perhaps should have written 'invested' in that last sentence, as those badges now cost much, much more on the likes of e-Bay today than I paid for them back then.

George Best
signed photograph.

Above left: Supporters Club badge.

Above right: Player tin badge.

Below left: Roger Byrne tin badge.

Below right: Plastic star badge.

Also purchased on that first visit to Old Trafford was a red and white United shoulder bag – another item that is still around today.

Over the course of time, other badges were to find their way into the collection, including a small tin badge with an image of Roger Byrne encircled by the words 'Roger Byrne Fan Club'. As far as I am aware, Roger didn't have a fan club. Neither did any of the other players of the period, so where did this item stem from?

Even more collectable, and expensive, are the red plastic star badges, produced no one knows where and sold on the approach streets to Old Trafford in the 1950s and early 1960s. There are other plastic badges from around the time out there, but the star ones are the most common.

Other examples of the badges out there include a lovely metal buttonhole badge with a horseshoe-shaped back, which was an official player badge from the mid-1950s. Club shop purchases included the Stretford End, Red Devils and the Stuart Pearson tin items.

Before moving on, I must add that many of the badges that were available back in the 1960s have been reproduced in recent times. A look on the reverse side for a name like 'Coffer' will keep you right, although the older ones can usually show a bit of aging, which also helps if you are looking to buy an original.

So, badges and autographs. We are now off on the magical mystery tour of all things collectable relating to Manchester United.

Let's just drift back to autographs for a moment. I used to collect them when I first started going to watch my local club, Queen of the South. I would sometimes run onto the pitch when the players came out just before kick-off, but normally waited on the opposition team bus to arrive. Any I missed then, I would get at full time. Only one player ever refused to sign and that was Celtic's Jimmy Johnstone. It was just him and I, but he said no.

Stuart Pearson, Red Devil and Stretford End tin badges, as well as a metal official badge.

Having said that, there was another in later years who refused to sign and that was Roy Keane. I waited for him pre-match one day at Old Trafford as I wanted him to sign the Footballer of the Year menu when he won it. He duly arrived, signed for a couple of other people, and when I asked 'Could I have your autograph please Roy?', he reached for the pen and the menu, but when he saw what it was he turned and walked away! He eventually did sign it when I visited Carrington on a Supporters Club trip.

Today, signed shirts are very popular, often carrying a price tag of a couple of hundred pounds and signed in an unidentifiable scrawl by a squad member. There are a number of reputable dealers out there, but such items are ignored by many of the old-school collectors who would rather have a signed item from a player of yesteryear. It must also be added that due to the signatures of today's players they are easy to forge, hence the reluctance of some to bother collecting them.

Like programmes, pre-war autographs are out there, but the likes of Billy Meredith's can put you back as much as one of the pre-war programmes. Everyone wants the signatures of the Busby Babes – in particular, that of Duncan Edwards – and many end up paying out more than they should as they are not overly rare, seeing as the players of that period seldom, if ever, refused an autograph. What is difficult to find is the signatures of all the Babes together, as you will nearly always find either Colman or Bent missing for some reason.

One of the countless items in the old United Souvenir Shop, which today would be a goldmine for collectors, was an A4 sized black and white photograph signed by the United

Billy Meredith autograph.

A signed album page from April 1951, with the signatures of some twenty-three players.

squad of 1965–6. Those photographs – all hand signed by the way, and not pre-stamped – were given to the players by the handful and they took them home to sign. They would then bring them back and pass them on to a teammate until everyone had signed. Having said that, I have one that is only partly signed. They must have gotten fed up!

One area of collecting I almost immediately moved into (when I became aware that the programme collecting was going nowhere due to those gaps being fewer and harder to fill) was match tickets. At the time, this was a collecting area that few bothered about. Some did collect tickets, but mainly from games that they or relatives went to. This was a big plus point really, as it allowed me to pick up some nice ones cheaply. Nowadays, it is the complete opposite, as it is a popular collecting diversity. Many who do not even class themselves as collectors make a point of keeping their match tickets from games they attend, particularly from their trips to the European aways.

Tickets are also very easy to store compared to programmes, with a small photograph album being ideal, as it allows you to put two tickets back to back in one pocket. Some of these albums come in a small open ended box, which allows you to arrange them in either season, or competition order, or even both, with details on the end for easy filing.

Unfortunately, however, the days of the paper ticket – or if you venture further back, those of light card – seem to be numbered, certainly for United home games, with the club having used the membership card as the match day ticket for the past few years. But thankfully, like programmes, there are hundreds out there to collect. Also like programmes, it is difficult to select just a handful for illustration purposes. I could have filled a whole book; selecting only a few is the difficult part.

Signed team photograph.

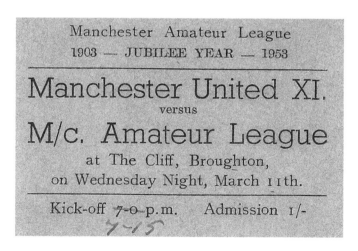

Manchester Amateur
League ticket.

There are rarities such as those from the early European aways, but the likes of the United XI versus a Manchester Amateur League side for a game played at The Cliff in 1953 is a real one-off and possibly one of the rarest I have seen.

Others that stand out in the collection are the likes of Chesterfield away in the final of the 1956 FA Youth Cup. This has 'complementary' stamped across it and reputedly belonged to one of the players, although which one it was I have no idea.

Still others include Arsenal away in 1957/58 – that last league game prior to Munich – and a flimsy, narrow piece of paper covering the first post-war FA Cup Tie against Nottingham Forest. Then there is a friendly against Portsmouth in Nigeria, when only around a dozen United supporters were present. Also shown are tickets for the

Above left: Chesterfield FA Youth Cup.

Above right: Arsenal ticket.

Below left: Nottingham Forest 1946 FA Cup ticket.

Below right Nigeria ticket.

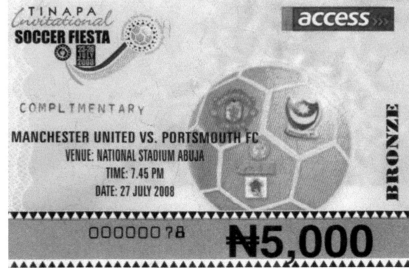

Lockerbie Disaster fund match against Queen of the South – a United fixture that for a change did not entail a twelve-hour round trip.

European ties are particularly collectable, especially from a memorable fixture such as Benfica away in 1966, or the Champions League Final of 1999.

Ground tickets for the early European ties (and also domestic cup ties) had a perforation down the centre, not simply spoiling the actual ticket, but often making

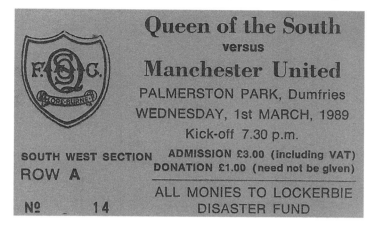

Queen of the South away ticket.

Right: Benfica away ticket.

Below: 1999 CL Final ticket.

MANCHESTER UNITED F.C. LTD.   N⍛ 26202

European Champion Clubs' Cup Competition
SEMI-FINAL TIE — SECOND LEG
MANCHESTER UNITED v. REAL MADRID
AT OLD TRAFFORD   KICK-OFF 7-15 p.m
THURSDAY, 25th APRIL, 1957

GROUNDSIDE

3/6 incl. tax   It is recommended that this ticket be presented at least 30 minutes before Kick-Off

Secretary

*In the event of the match being postponed through circumstances beyond
control, this ticket will be available for the re-arranged date.*
NO MONEY RETURNED.
KEEP THIS PORTION   TO BE GIVEN UP

Above: Real Madrid EC home ticket.

Below: Postponed match ticket.

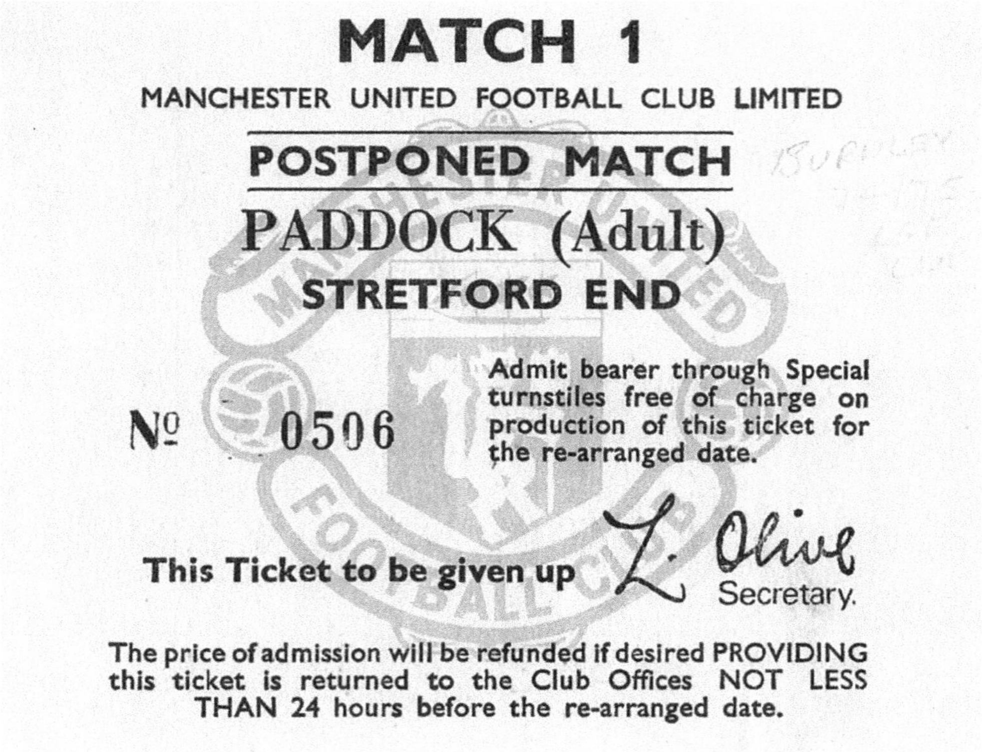

MATCH 1
MANCHESTER UNITED FOOTBALL CLUB LIMITED

POSTPONED MATCH
PADDOCK (Adult)
STRETFORD END

N⍛ 0506

Admit bearer through Special
turnstiles free of charge on
production of this ticket for
the re-arranged date.

This Ticket to be given up

Secretary.

The price of admission will be refunded if desired PROVIDING
this ticket is returned to the Club Offices NOT LESS
THAN 24 hours before the re-arranged date.

it difficult to know exactly what match it was issued for. There was no such problem with the illustration of the Real Madrid European Cup semi-final second leg tie at Old Trafford in 1957, however, as this one was never used.

To make a ticket collection somewhat different, you could also include the one for the Stretford End Paddock, which was given out when you entered the ground on 27 January 1967 for the match against Arsenal, as the game was in some doubt and was eventually called off due to heavy fog The ticket given out enabled you to gain admission free of charge on the re-arranged date.

Another unusual type of ticket is a 'complementary' one, given to someone on 13 February 1960 and allowing admission to the Stretford End.

Season tickets do not have the same appeal as match tickets, although those from the pre-war era and the immediate post-war period are certainly more collectable, and indeed much better to look at than the plastic items of today. Collecting-wise, you can actually end up with a couple of different ones for some seasons as United issued both Gents and Ladies season tickets.

Above left: Complimentary ticket.

Above right: Pre-war season ticket.

Chapter 4

Take a Card

The pre-war period was something that – collecting-wise at least – didn't really interest me or grasp my attention too much in those early days. Moving away from programmes there were now several new doors opening, one of those having a heavy pre-war presence – cigarette cards.

Cigarette cards, rather ironically, began to appear around the same time as the fledgling Newton Heath Football Club, so there are countless cards out there to collect. Note, however, that some of those early cards can sell for the price of a ticket to a Premier League fixture (and sometimes more), but on a plus point United collectors, for once, are not charged more than those of other clubs, mainly due to the fact that Newton Heath were still ranked among the also-rans in the football world and none of their players featured on cigarette cards except in the colours of another club. So while you are saving money, you need to know your history to find the 'Heathen' players among the numerous cards from those bygone days. One such example is the Harry Errentz card shown here, which was issued by Ogdens in 1901, when Errentz was a Tottenham Hotspur player.

Cigarette cards continued to be popular up until the Second World War years, with countless sets featuring the footballers of the day being issued by companies such

Harry Errentz cigarette card.

as Copes, Taddy, Cohen Weenan and Gallaher, and as United grew in strength, their players were featured on a more regular basis. It was not, however, just head and shoulder images of the star players of the day, such as Meredith and Roberts, that were to feature on those cards, as the excellent Pattreiouex set featured action shots and team groups, giving you an excellent photographic history.

For those wanting to build not simply a collection of Manchester United-related cigarette cards but a photographic history of players who represented the club, the Godfrey Phillips Pinnace cards, of which some 2,462 were issued between 1920 and 1924, featured countless 'unfamiliar' individuals who pulled on the red shirt, albeit listed under a variety of different clubs. Again you have to know your history, or have the likes of Garth Dykes' *The United Alphabet* included in your United collection. This would allow you to identify players who represented United with other clubs.

Those Pinnace cards, which show a nice head and shoulders photograph of the player, measured a mere 3.5 x 4.5 cm, but if you collected twenty-five cards you could exchange them for a larger card of a similar style.

Above left: Charlie Roberts cigarette card.

Above middle: George Stacey cigarette card.

Above right: Patr'x card.

Right: George Wall cigarette card.

The featured card is that of Bill Inglis, then of Raith Rovers but later to become a member of Matt Busby's backroom staff.

I mentioned a few lines back that Newton Heath players fail to appear in cigarette card form under the club name, but you can find some 'Heathens' in the superb, and often very expensive Baines cards. These cards, usually shield shaped, measured approximately 8–9 cm x 6–7 cm and were issued by John Baines of Bradford between the mid-1880s and 1920 and illustrated a wide variety of subjects.

But soon the cigarette card had a challenger in the world of collectables – the picture postcard, an instant form of communication which sprang to the fore at the start of the twentieth century, with millions produced featuring every conceivable subject and scenes from arguably every town and village in Britain.

1902 saw the somewhat financially troubled Newton Heath change its name to Manchester United, hoping that such a move would also bring a change of fortune, and a year later came the first Manchester United postcard. Issued in 1903, the postcard shows the Imperial Hotel, which was once an imposing structure on London Road, a short walk from Piccadilly station. This, however, was no ordinary drinking place with accommodation.

In the dark, dismal days of the early 1900s, club captain Harry Stafford was much involved in fundraising for the impoverished Newton Heath and employed his St Bernard, Major, in his efforts. The dog, with a collection box around his neck, wandered off and into a pub owned by brewery businessman John H. Davis and was subsequently brought back to his owner with Davies expressing an interest in buying it for his daughter. Stafford agreed to sell, but only if Davies would invest in his club. An agreement was reached and Davies, who owned the Imperial Hotel, among others in the city, became something of a saviour.

Above left: Pinnace card.

Above right: Farman Baines card.

The hotel became the club headquarters and Stafford had his portrait displayed on the outer wall. He was actually gifted the pub by Davies in 1901, but didn't last long behind the pumps, declaring that this was not the life for him!

The 1909 FA Cup success also brought a flurry of postcards, ranging from match action to the victorious homecoming at Manchester Central station. Match action, or indeed simply photographs of the cloth-capped crowd, appeared frequently on postcards, but it is the pre-war team groups and images of individual players that capture the imagination of the present day collector, the same team group often appearing in a different format from a different source. They do make a superb collecting avenue, but beware, many of them do not come cheap.

Illustrated here is a postcard showing the triumphant 1909 cup winning side returning home from London, sitting proudly on a horse and cart as they leave Manchester's Central station. Captain Charlie Roberts can be seen to the front holding the trophy.

The team group, with the players sporting a white shirt with a (red) 'V', is dated *c.* 1924–25 and shows what is now K stand and the area for the away supporters in the background. If you look really closely, you can see the wording 'Manchester United' along the top of the wall in the top centre of the photograph.

Before leaving postcards, there are a couple of other samples to throw into the equation. First is a selection postcard sent to an Arnold Banton during the 1947/48 season, telling him that he had been selected to play on a particular date and where and when to attend. The second is a postcard sent by the club to supporters telling them that they had been successful with their application in obtaining a ticket for the 1963 FA Cup Final. Similar postcards can be found for the 1968 European Cup Final and others.

As you have read, my own United collection had kicked off with the bubble gum-related trade cards and this section continued to increase as in the years passed by. Cards were continuously issued in packets of sweet cigarettes and with chewing

Right: Imperial Hotel postcard.

Below: Victorious FA Cup winners return home, 1909.

Team postcard, 1924/25.

Manchester United Football Club, Ltd.

TELEPHONE: 1661 TRAfford Park.
Telegraphic Address: "Stadium, Manchester."

OLD TRAFFORD,
MANCHESTER, 16.

Secretary : : W. CRICKMER

6ᵗ Match

Date as Postmark

Dear Sir,

You are selected to play in the match *United*

versus *Gardners* at *Clevely Playing Fields Winton*

on *Sat.* next, Kick off at *3. 0* o'clock prompt.

Train or 'Bus leaves *Meet Manchester Cathedral 1.45*

If unable to play, please let me know per return.

Yours truly, W. CRICKMER.

Won 5 - 1 'Played LH

Player selection card.

gum, and also in the numerous comics that had appeared in the newsagents since the 1920s, when boys' reading material came to the fore, with the likes of *Champion, Topical Times, Boys Magazine, Adventure* and *Wizzard* all making their debut, followed in the 1930s by similar titles such as *Hotspur*.

Other pre-war publications like the short-lived *Daily Citizen*, which ran between 1912 and 1915, and *All Sports*, dated between 1919 and 1930, issued A4 sized team groups, as illustrated here. Not many will have survived, but they are well worth looking out for.

While it could be said that the cigarette card encouraged smoking, those comics and magazines could be said to be little more than a 'bribe' to purchase the various publications in order for the youngsters to get the cards. Those publications,

Right: Cup final ticket application success card.

Below: *Daily Citizen* team group.

MANCHESTER UNITED FOOTBALL CLUB
OLD TRAFFORD ———————— MANCHESTER, 16

May, 1963.

Dear Supporter,
    Replying to your application, I am very pleased to forward a ticket for the F.A. Cup Final. I trust you will have an enjoyable outing and that you will see an excellent game with a most satisfactory result.
    Many thanks for your continued support which is very much appreciated by all at Old Trafford.

Yours sincerely,

L. Olive
Secretary.

N.B.—This card is a receipt for tokens withdrawn and must be presented in accordance with a Press announcement in the event of a replay.

Supplement to "THE DAILY CITIZEN."

1913. MANCHESTER UNITED FOOTBALL CLUB. 1914.

Copyright Photo.]   [MACK & Co., MANCHESTER.

Top Row: ASST. TRAINER   W. MEREDITH   G. WALL   R. H. BEALE   F. KNOWLES   T. CHORLON   TAYLOR (*Trainer*)
Second Row: T. GIBBS   M. HAMILL   A. TURNBULL   G. STACEY   R. DUCKWORTH   E. J. WEST   G. ANDERSON
Bottom Row: W. WOODCOCK   A. WHALLEY   J. HODGE   A. HOOPER

A P. Co., Ltd   "THE DAILY CITIZEN" FOOTBALL CARTOONS AND CRITICISMS ARE THE REAL THING.

along with the likes of card-producing Chix, A&BC and Barratt, gave the collector plenty to look for.

Perhaps the most difficult card set to find, and indeed complete, was issued by the *News Chronicle Daily Despatch* and was given away on match days outside Old

Above: *All Sports* team group.

Below: Trade cards.

Trafford *c.* 1956. The United set consists of fifteen players, with the likes of John Doherty, Colin Webster and Geoff Bent featuring alongside the more familiar Duncan Edwards, Roger Byrne and Tommy Taylor.

All those cards could be enhanced by the depicted player's signature, as could the modern-day cards that were to saturate the market in countless different formats from

NEWS CHRONICLE AND DISPATCH
POCKET PORTRAIT

DAVE PEGG
Manchester United F.C.

Right: News Chronicle card.

Below: Trade cards.

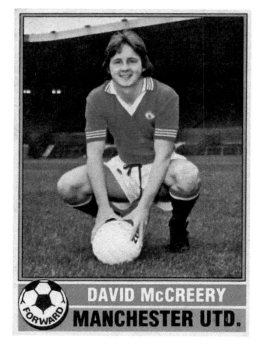

DAVID McCREERY
MANCHESTER UTD.

DAVID BECKHAM

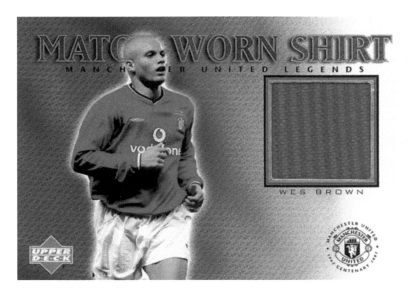

Trade card.

the likes of Match Attax, Pro-Set and Panini, offering everything from limited edition issues to ones containing a small square of a match worn shirt! Somehow, they all lack the style and attraction of those from the 1950s and '60s.

There is a veritable Aladdin's Cave of United memorabilia out there, but before delving into the filing cabinet to see what materialises from those box files, let's look at diversifying away from the beaten track, which is something that can add a different dimension to the collection.

Chapter 5

A Collecting Diversion

Moving away from Manchester United as a whole, you could build something of a mini-collection around various individuals such as Sir Matt Busby, Sir Alex Ferguson, George Best, Ryan Giggs, Eric Cantona and the legendary Duncan Edwards.

The latter of course appears on numerous cards, but there are many collectors out there who seek out programmes covering his representative games; not simply his full England international games, but those as a schoolboy with the England under 23s, as well as 'B' side, the Football League and, not to be forgotten, the Army.

DUNCAN EDWARDS

Above: Duncan Edwards card.

Right: Team page from Duncan Edwards's first schoolboy international programme.

TEAMS

ENGLAND
(White)

1
A. J. SILVER
(Maidenhead)

2
J. WOODWARD
(Islington)

3
J. F. MIDDLEMASS
(E. Northumberland)

4
P. R. MARTON
(York)

5
M. UNDERWOOD
(Kettering)

6
W. P. OLDHAM
(Ellesmere Port)

7
H. COLLIER
(Horwich)

8
A. FARRELL
(Wirral)

9
D. EDWARDS
(Dudley)

10
R. PARRY (Capt.)
(Derby)

11
D. PEGG
(Doncaster)

English Reserves : P. SHACKLETON (Todmorden), J. RANKIN (Aldershot),
G. JONES (Crewe), R. E. BARNES (Bath).

Referee : Mr. A. C. REED (Cardiff).
Linesmen : Mr. L. CALLAGHAN (Merthyr Tydfil), Mr. W. BEEKS (Tredegar).

Irish Reserves : J. STRAIN (Belfast), W. RODGERS (Belfast), E. DUBOIS (Belfast).

11
G. MURRAY
(Lisburn)

10
W. J. HIGGINSON
(Lisburn)

9
R. ADAIR
(Belfast)

8
J. HILL
(Carrickfergus)

7
T. JENKINS
(Ballyclare)

6
F. McGUIRE
(Lambeg)

5
S. F. LARMOUR
(Bangor) (Capt.)

4
A. LUKE
(Ballymena)

3
L. TORRANS
(Belfast)

2
D. ALEXANDER
(Ballymena)

1
T. BALMER
(Coleraine)

IRELAND
(Green)

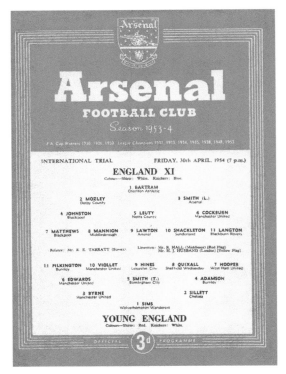

Above left: Duncan Edwards programme.

Above right: Photograph from the order of service for the unveiling of the Duncan Edwards windows.

One of the most collectable items is the order of service for the unveiling of the stained glass windows in St Francis's Church, Dudley, a short walk from his former home. This is a lovely little item and contains an actual black and white photograph of the two windows, one of which shows Duncan in his United kit, the other in the white of England.

There are also a number of modern-day collectables relating to Duncan, which keep his memory alive, like my own invite to the unveiling of his statue in Dudley town centre.

A Sir Alex Ferguson collection can encompass both sides of the border through his playing and managerial career, while his career at Old Trafford requires no in-depth study. From the latter, you could have his last programme as a manager at West Bromwich Albion, or items from his testimonial, or from being made Freeman of Manchester. Move across Hadrian's Wall and there are his triumphs with Aberdeen, or his playing career with the likes of Rangers, Ayr United, St Johnstone or Queens Park, along with playing cards depicting him in his playing days. He was also in later years to receive the Freedom of both Glasgow and Aberdeen, so there is much to seek out and collect.

In relation to Sir Matt Busby, you can, like Sir Alex Ferguson, drift back to his playing career for items such as programmes with Liverpool, Manchester City and Scotland. There are cards from his City days, while his time with United produced countless menus, and of course the order of service from his funeral.

Duncan Edwards statue.

Sir Alex Ferguson card.

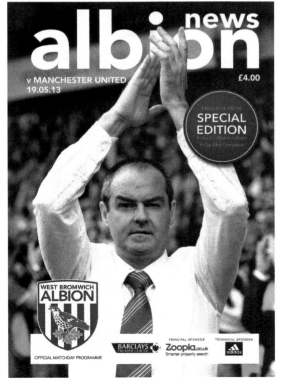

Above: Team page from Sir Alex Ferguson's Queen's Park debut.

Left: Programme cover for Sir Alex Ferguson's last game in charge of United.

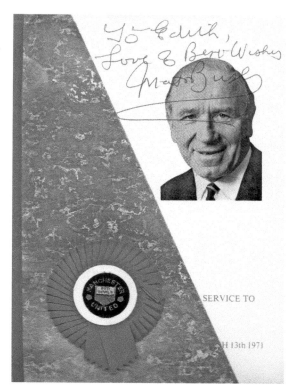

M. BUSBY.
Manchester City F.C.
TOPICAL
TIMES.

Sir Matt Busby.

George Best, on the other hand, can be a collector's dream, with innumerable cards, programmes, magazines and everything in between, including jigsaws. Following his death I produced a special 'United Collectors Club' newsletter, as I did for Sir Matt Busby, and it was simply a case of what to leave out, rather than what to include, as there was just so much out there.

Here I have included the order of service from his funeral, which I obtained from his sister, the front of the menu when he won Footballer of the Year in 1968 (made even more collectable as it is signed not just by George, but also by Bobby Charlton, Bobby Moore and Alf Ramsey), a large plastic figure produced by Mettoy and a special issue £5 note.

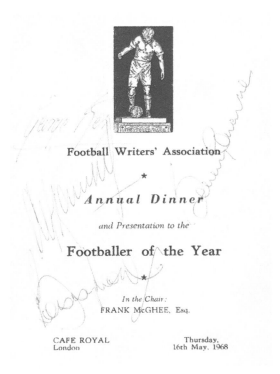

Football Writers' Association

*

Annual Dinner

and Presentation to the

Footballer of the Year

*

In the Chair:
FRANK McGHEE, Esq.

CAFE ROYAL   Thursday,
London   16th May, 1968

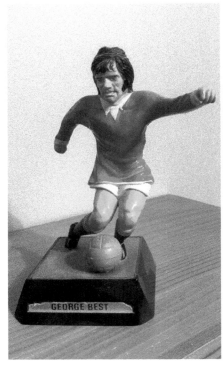

George Best.

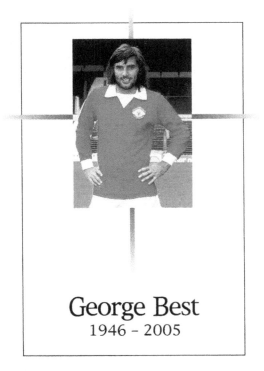

George Best
1946 – 2005

Eric Cantona.

As for stars of the modern era, let's pick out two from United's vast array of talented individuals – Eric Cantona and Ryan Giggs. Again, you can build up a mini-collection on those two individuals, and it is one again difficult to simply select two or three items, but kicking off with the French maverick, I have selected a figurine, upturned collar and all, an advertising postcard issued by Nike and a couple of items from when he was voted Footballer of the Year.

Equally difficult to select for inclusion were items relating to Ryan Giggs, the most decorated player in football history. Born in Wales but brought up in the Salford area

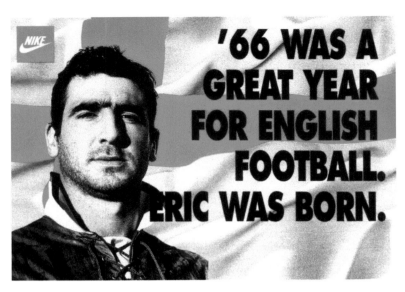

Eric Cantona
postcard.

of Manchester, where better to start than with a match programme from his days with Salford Schools, this one against St Helens at Old Trafford in May 1989, when he was then known as Ryan Wilson. Next comes an item from when he was given the Freedom of Salford in January 2010.

But let's now return to everything United as there are still a thousand and one things to cover.

City of Salford Schools' Football Association

SALFORD

ST. HELENS

E.S.F.A. Trophy Final 2nd Leg

at Old Trafford
(By kind permission Manchester United F.C.)

Thursday 18th May 1989
Kick-off 7.00 p.m.

Programme 30p

Ryan Giggs.

Special Meeting of Salford City Council

Thursday 7 January, 2010
The Lowry, Salford Quays

*Service To Celebrate
The Life
Of*

David George Herd

15ᵗʰ April 1934 - 1ˢᵗ October 2016

Service held on
Friday 14ᵗʰ October 2016
at
The Parish Church of Middlebie in Dumfries & Galloway
Followed by Committal at Middlebie Cemetery
Conducted by Miss Jeanette Wilson, Lay Minister

Freedom of the City of Salford

Ryan Joseph Giggs, OBE

Above left: Ryan Giggs.

Above right: David Herd service sheet.

Something that many might find rather morbid, but others consider very collectable, are funeral order of service sheets. Along with the aforementioned George Best one, others have also found their way into the collection, like that of David Herd.

The latter was obtained personally, as I found out the night prior to the funeral that it was to be held locally and I managed to attend – the only non-family member to do so, I must add.

A number of these order of services tend not to mention that the person ever played football, never mind for United, but David's carried three photographs on the inside page, and contained on page three the club crests of the four clubs he had played for and the crest of the Scottish international side. There was, however, a rather strange surprise on the inside of the back cover.

Here there was a small piece of paper stapled for you to send your memories of David to the family and underneath I had noticed a nice black and white shot of David in his United Cup Final kit. However, when I got home and my daughter asked to see the service sheet, I noticed when she lifted up the piece of paper it had a photograph of David in his Stoke colours. Puzzled, as I was sure that I had seen the '63 Cup Final shirt, I checked again and sure enough I had. As I had picked up another order of service upon leaving, since I thought someone would want it, I checked this one, only to find that it contained a coloured shot of David in an ordinary United shirt. Unusual, but nice.

Chapter 6

Menus, the Printed Word and Relics of a Bygone Age

One of those collecting areas I particularly enjoy is that of menus; not that I enjoy eating, but due to the fact they are attractive to look at and more often than not commemorate a special game or occasion in the club's history. Some can be simple four-page card items, while others might have a four-page insert detailing how the evening in question might progress.

European fixtures would see both teams get together in a city centre hotel for an after-match meal and a few drinks, and many of the menus from those fixtures, when appearing on the marketplace today, are signed by various players and individuals. One of the prized items in my collection comes from the European Cup Tie against Dukla Prague in 1957 and is signed by members of both teams, with the unusual addition of Molly Leach, the girlfriend of Duncan Edwards, and also that of Jean Busby.

Dukla Prague menu.

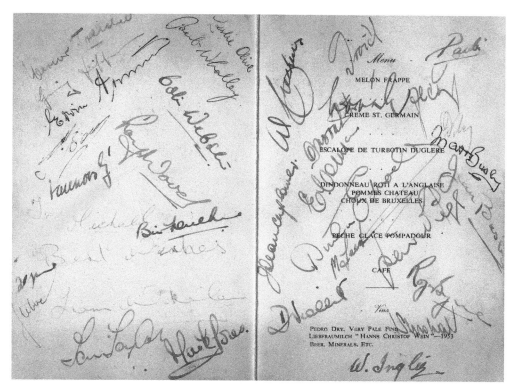

The signed inside of the menu.

The menu from the celebrations following the 1968 European Cup Final is quite unique, as it has the actual result on the front. Considering the game went into extra time and the lack of modern technology, someone must have earned a bit on overtime that night.

From the opening of the United Museum comes another menu signed by a few well-known names, including Pele, who never played for United, unfortunately, while perhaps one of the most unusual menus in the collection is that for the Denis Irwin testimonial dinner, which comes in a CD case!

You have bought, or been given this book, so perhaps you have a small collection of United titles. To collect every one published you would require a good two or three bookcases as United in the printed form is quite substantial and I suppose I have contributed to those numerous titles in a small way.

There are numerous good books on the club and its players. On the other hand, there are also a considerable number that would be best forgotten about. I am not going list either here, but simply point out one or two that certainly do merit a place on the United bookshelf.

The United correspondent with the *Manchester Evening Chronicle* was Alf Clarke and he produced the first club history in book form in 1951. Although not a blow-by-blow account, this softback book with an eye-catching cover is still an interesting and informative read. Clarke also wrote what could be best described as a booklet three years earlier in a 'Famous Football Clubs' series.

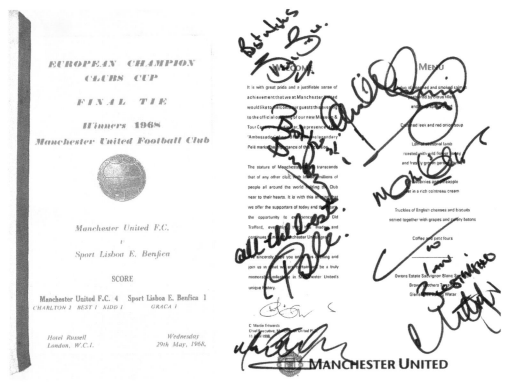

Above left: 1968 European Cup Final menu.

Above right: The signed menu for the opening of the museum.

Denis Irwin menu.

Above left: Alf Clarke's *Manchester United* book from the 'Famous Football Clubs' series.

Above right: Alf Clarke's booklet, 'Official History of Manchester United'.

Also very collectable are David Meek's *Manchester United Football Books*, which began in the late 1960s and carried on into the mid-1970s. David was the much-respected United man at the *Manchester Evening News* for a considerable number of years, making his books an enjoyable read.

A couple of other titles well worth trying to obtain, if you haven't already got them that is, are *Champions Again* by Ralph Finn and Tom Tyrell's *Manchester United, the Religion* and *Red Devils Disciples*.

Newspapers, although often large and somewhat bulky to store, are real historical items and are, along with the match reports they contain, for me at least a major collecting avenue, and one that has been hugely beneficial to me when writing my books. I have kept match reports and cuttings for some considerable time now, and although the newspaper reports of today are a far cry from those of two or three decades ago, they relate the history of the club like no other item of memorabilia can.

Quite often someone who had attended a particular match would insert a match report into the programme; others would compile scrapbooks, using notebooks or whatever to glue the reports into. Many, however, would keep complete newspapers, like a gentleman from Gorton who was brought to my attention back in the 1980s as I was told he had 'some old newspapers' and was prepared to sell them. Contact was made and it turned out that he had more or less every *Manchester Evening Chronicle* Saturday 'Pink' from around 1950 to 1961 and every *Manchester Evening News* Saturday 'Green' from around 1954 to 1961, plus other odd issues. Unfortunately, none covered Munich, as my 'informant' had already taken those. It took two trips

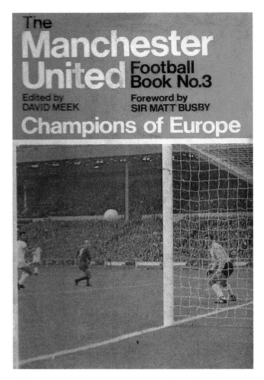

Above left: David Meek's *The Manchester United Football Book*.

Above right: Ralph Finn's *Champions Again: Manchester United*.

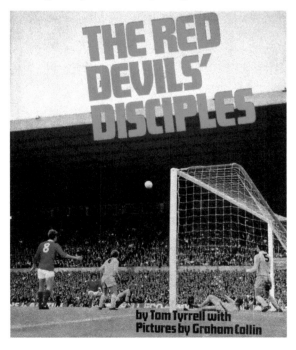

Tom Tyrell's *The Devils' Disciples*.

Manchester Evening Chronicle newspaper.

to his house on a match day to get them all, having to return to Victoria station and leave them in the left luggage department, but it was all worth it, as they worked out at about 30p each if I remember rightly.

A big seller back in the 1950s, 1960s and for a short while in the 1970s, were special souvenir editions before they became few and far between, later to disappear altogether. These were produced to cover an important fixture such as a Cup Final, or semi-final, or indeed any game seen as worthy of some newsprint being used up by the local newspaper. In Manchester, certainly up to the '60s, the collector was often spoilt, as both the *Evening News* and the *Chronicle* would issue 'specials' for the same match.

In more recent times, some have found newspapers to be something of a money-making machine, bringing home foreign issues covering United games in Europe (and beyond). These are then sold at well above face value, paying for the odd beer or two while away. Many will purchase those editions, although perhaps not because they collect newspapers as such, but because no match programme was issued, and if there is a pitch diagram with the teams listed, they consider this to be an ideal substitute.

Those foreign publications, such as against Real Madrid in 1957 and 1968, when no programmes were issued, are very collectable, as are those from the 1999 Champions League run and in particular the final itself, with some quality issues from Germany and Spain covering the game in Barcelona. The after-match issues are well worth having, with the 'Sport' issue from the following day devoting some twenty-three pages to the game.

There are also a considerable number of foreign magazines out there, issued prior to and after games, and they are certainly worth looking for. Two I have cover the

Above left: *Manchester Evening Chronicle* souvenir issue.

Above right: *Arriba*, a newspaper published in Madrid, from 1957.

Left: *Sport* newspaper from the 1999 CL Final.

Sportowiec magazine.

1967/68 European Cup Tie against Gornik, which are copies of the Polish sports magazine *Sportowiec* and are dated 5 March and 19 March, numbers 10 and 12 or alternatively numbers 901 and 903. Strangely, the former is priced dearer than the latter.

The earliest of the two issues covers the Old Trafford first leg tie, but only with five photographs on the back page, while the other issue, covering the match in a snow-swept Poland, devotes the centre pages to the game with six photographs and five paragraphs of text. One of the photographs shows the backs of nine players lined up on the United goal line defending a free kick, while another shows three United defenders and two Gornik players challenging for the same ball near the United goal.

Where I obtained those magazines from, I have no idea, but I do think they came from their country of origin.

If it is the written word that you enjoy, then you are really spoilt for choice, as there are countless booklets and magazines out there. You could kick off with Supporters Club handbooks, which were prominent in the 1960s. The *League Championship Souvenir Handbook* of 1965–66 contained a look back at the season with statistics and countless photographs of the players, along with the reserve and junior teams and match action. There is also a potted history of the club. The 1967–68 one is smaller in size, but is again plentiful on statistics, photographs and articles, including one on Duncan Edwards.

Above left: Manchester United handbook, 1965/66.

Above right: Manchester United handbook, 1967/68.

The Second Division championship success of 1975 saw the publication of a sixty-four-page colourful booklet by Canonbury Publishing Company in London, entitled 'Salute to Manchester United – Welcome to Gloryland', which contained some excellent photographs of the players of the period along with some historical content.

From the Cup Finals of 1948 and 1963 came the official player brochures, which were produced in the hope of raising a few pounds to supplement the meagre wages of the time. The 1948 one consists of twenty pages, with photographs, player pen pictures and articles, while that of 1963 contains forty-eight pages and, although containing countless articles, is worth having.

There was also another player-produced brochure in 1957 to cover the challenge for the European Cup, FA Cup League and Championship treble. This consists of forty pages and, although heavy on advertisements, has photographs and pen pictures of all the players and quite often turns up with the team group in the centre pages containing one or two signatures.

Staying with the 1948 final for a minute or two, there are one or two really collectable little booklets relating to the match against Blackpool, which saw United lift the trophy following a 4-2 victory, such as 'The Daily Dispatch Cup Final Souvenir', the 'Sport' Cup Final souvenir, which is arguably the best, and 'A Lancashire Wembley'.

The 'Daily Dispatch' issue is a mere eight pages. Articles on both clubs, how they got to the final, team groups, pen pictures and a couple of other photographs make up this publication. The 'Sport' produced issue consists of twenty pages of articles and

Right: Division Two booklet.

Below: 1948 players' brochure.

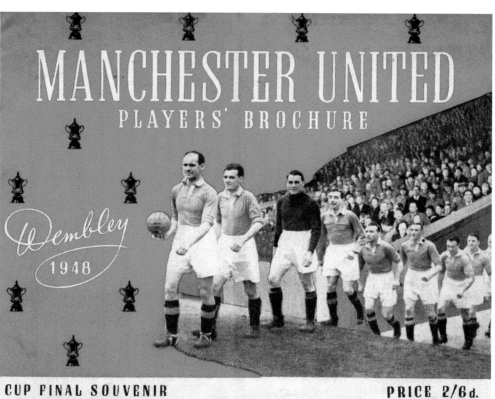

1963 players' brochure.

1957 players' brochure.

photographs, while the 'Lancashire Wembley' publication consists of sixteen pages and tells you everything you want to know about the final, including the best way to get to Wembley once you are in London and an article on where the Cup Final tickets go.

The likes of *Charles Buchan's Football Monthly*, *Soccer Star* and other publications of the time like *Sport Express* also produced excellent FA Cup Final souvenir issues, the former also publishing a special on Denis Law, while in the pre-war *Topical Times* you can find some superb articles on the club and its players, with United manager A. Scott Duncan penning a series of articles on his life in football and the legendary Louis Rocca also recalling his involvement in the game.

Charles Buchan's Football Monthly also produced the excellent 'Salute to Manchester United', which was published in 1959. With sixty-four pages of text and photographs, it is a worthwhile addition to any collection, and was published at a time when items like this were few and far between, making this something that would have been well received by United supporters of the period.

Just a flick through the pages takes you back to a bygone age and not just through the excellent photographs, but also via the adverts with a United rosette with a 'new emblem of entirely original design, depicting a Red Devil' available for 1*s* 3*d,* plus 3*d* postage. On the same page is an advert for David Stacey's Football Programmes,

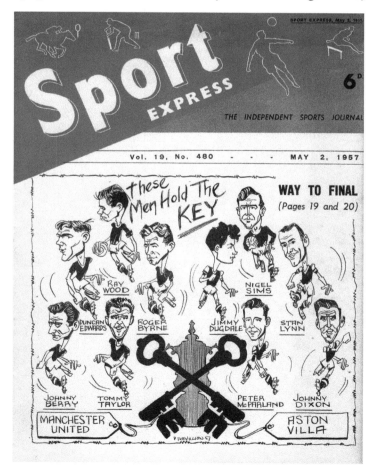

1957 Cup Final edition of *Sport Express.*

while there is a small advert for copies of the Feyenoord–United friendly programme from the Phillips Programme Shop in Wythenshawe, Manchester, priced at 2*s*, post free. There are other programme adverts, along with 'Bobby Charlton football boots', 'Boots by Matt Busby', 'Umbro football kit styled by Matt Busby' and even one for 'Books for Adult Reading'!

Charles Buchan booklet from 1959.

While mentioning the excellent *Charles Buchan* publication, among the numerous adverts in their 1950s editions you could send away for black and white postcard sized photographs of players from every team in the Football League, and I think I am right in saying that they came in both head and shoulders and an action shot. The United ones did at least. Today, those photographs are quite difficult to come by and I was extremely fortunate to obtain an almost complete set in one go. An excellent shot of Liam Whelan is shown here.

Other publications well worth seeking out are *Sport/Sport Express* due to the team photographs on the front pages, *World Sports* and the *FA News*, all of which included good United content now and again. The *FA News* for instance included a nice Munich tribute following the disaster.

While on Cup Finals, how about delving back to yesteryear for the good old-fashioned song sheet, from a time when songs/chanting from the crowd were, excuse the pun, unheard of. The only singing at this time took place pre-match, with popular refrains of the day lead by a gentleman on a high stand alongside a military band.

Charles Buchan photograph of Liam Whelan.

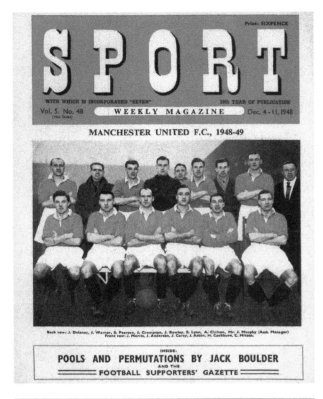

Sport magazine.

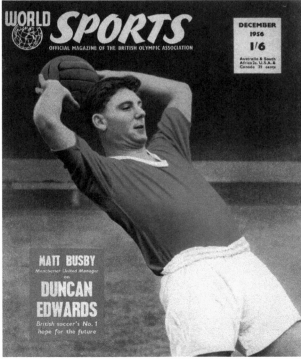

World Sports magazine.

Another relic of yesteryear, and something of a 'must have' item when it came to dress attire, more so for Cup Finals, although not as compulsory as the good old flat cap, is the rosette. This is most certainly another item from a bygone age, and more often than not rather primitive to the eye, but nevertheless they do find their way into collections. Made by the dozens in back street premises at a cost of pennies, they were a profitable seller for the swagmen of old and a much better long-term investment than the current day half-and-half scarves. Many were simply coloured cloth with a piece of card bearing the name of a team stapled onto it. Some had a small replica of the FA Cup attached, no matter what fixture they were being sold at, while others might have a footballer attached in a close resemblance to a particular team's colours.

Rosettes are now a thing of the past, dying out in the 1970s, with many more than likely not even making the after-match journey home due to the purchaser's team being beaten and the rosette discarded in disgust; or perhaps it simply fell off on the packed terracing. No matter what, it is still collectable today. The image shown here is from the 1948 FA Cup Final.

1957 FA Cup Final song sheet.

Rosette from the 1948 FA
Cup Final.

Another somewhat relic from the golden age of football is the fixture card, although some clubs do continue to issue them; more so the smaller ones, as their fixtures seldom, if ever, change from the day they are announced.

Back in the pre- and immediate post-war eras, those fixture cards would more often than not be produced by a local newspaper, a shop, company, or public house, or more commonly a cigarette company like W. D. & H. O. Wills or Players, mainly as a form of advertising. Some would be issued to cover two local teams and were often plain to look at, but those issued by the cigarette companies would normally have a nice illustration of a footballer on the front. Having said that, I have one from 1959/60 that was produced by Ashburton Chemical Works of Trafford Park, and as well as United and City's fixtures there are two pages of tips for safety in the workplace!

Finding such cards in mint condition can be quite a task as more often than not those that have survived the tests of time have had the scores filled in. This is not a big deal I suppose, but the blank ones do look better.

1927-8

FOOTBALL
FIXTURE CARD

**BOLTON WANDERERS
MANCHESTER CITY
MANCHESTER UNITED**

With the
compliments
of
W.D.&H.O.WILLS.

BRANCH OF THE IMPERIAL TOBACCO CO (OF GREAT BRITAIN AND IRELAND) LIMITED

Fixture cards.

Chapter 7

Anything and Everything

From the past, back to the present and something that for some unknown reason has failed to generate the appeal of countless other collectables, certainly from the majority of collectors I know who collect United memorabilia, is the first day cover. Colourful and easy to store, they commemorate memorable fixtures or events, so what more could you ask for? But despite having so many plus points and certainly looking good with a signature or two added, the first day cover remains something of a 'no-go' area for some collectors, akin to that of signed shirts, which can also have little in the way of appeal.

The first day covers, like their collection companion in cards, lack that special appeal, perhaps because of their somewhat repetitiveness and looking very much identical. But as mentioned, as they are issued for certain fixtures that can turn out to become monumental in the history of Manchester United, they are well worth adding to a collection if signed by the goal scorer or goal scorers, or even the manager from that particular fixture.

There must have been hundreds of first day covers produced over the years, but I have simply picked out just two for illustration purposes. Shown here is one of the earlier examples and was issued for the 1968 European Cup Final. They can be found with different signatures, such as Busby, Best and Eusebio. The Busby one I have was one of a number found by pure chance, not by me I must add, in a second-hand shop in London. Alongside is one that commemorates the 1999 Champions League Final against Bayern Munich. It is postmarked in Barcelona and signed by Ole Gunnar Solskjær.

Football today is all about money, with the actual ninety minutes out on the pitch often of secondary importance. Instead of being run by football people, it is now the plaything of foreign owners with little thought to the long-standing supporter, while their business is run from nearer to home by accountants, who are again more interested in the bottom line than the score line. In years gone by no one could ever have imagined the vast amount of money that Manchester United would be worth today, nor the figures that would be added up following each home fixture and indeed every other day of the week.

With all that in mind, copies of the United accounts as sent to club shareholders prior to AGMs are yet another branch of that huge collecting tree. Arguably, there is not much in the way of interest in looking at a couple of columns of figures, but those accounts from the pre-war days make good and certainly interesting reading, shining a light on how football used to be all those years ago. They could also, of course, be considered items of historic interest.

EUROPEAN CUP FINAL
MANCHESTER UNITED
versus
BENFICA F.C., LISBON

WEMBLEY STADIUM
WEDNESDAY 29 MAY 1968

commemorative cover

Rembrandt Philatelics,
26 Park View,
Botley, Hants, SO3 2EF

First day cover, 1968 EC Final.

OFFICIAL FOOTBALL
COVER SERIES
SEASON 1998-99 No. 5N
THE 17th SERIES

MANCHESTER UNITED
THE EUROPEAN
CHAMPIONS' CUP
FINAL
VERSUS
BAYERN MUNICH

<u>MATCH RESULT</u>
MANCHESTER Utd ... 2   BAYERN MUNICH... 1
Sheringham   Basler
Solskjaer

Manchester United scored twice in the last minute to
clinch the European Championship and win the unique
"Treble" (League Championship & F.A. Cup too)

MANCHESTER UNITED
FOOTBALL CLUB
OLD TRAFFORD
MANCHESTER M16 0RA

First day cover, 1999 CL Final.

Manchester United Football Club, Limited.

Revenue Accounts

Seasons 1924-25 & 1925-26

AND

Balance Sheets

AS ON

May 9th, 1925 and May 8th, 1926.

NOTICE IS HEREBY GIVEN that the ANNUAL GENERAL MEETING of this Company will be held in the EXCHANGE HOTEL, FENNEL STREET, MANCHESTER, on THURSDAY, 23rd SEPTEMBER, 1926, at 7-0 p.m.

Agenda:

Minutes of Last Annual Meeting.
Directors' Report.
Balance Sheets and Accounts.
Election of Directors.
Election of Auditors.
Any other Business.

J. A. CHAPMAN,
Secretary.

Warwick Road,
Old Trafford, Manchester.
14th September, 1926.

(The place of Meeting has been arranged to suit convenience of Shareholders.)

Mr. ....

No. .... *Votes.*

This Report must be presented at the door for Admission.

Hutton, Hartley & Co. Ltd., Printers, Victoria St., Manchester

Accounts from 1925/26.

One of the reasons that I personally wanted to become a shareholder was to obtain the account statements, collectable items in their own right, and of course to have my name on a share certificate, which is another collectable item. When the current owners took over the club, everyone had to sell their shares and return their certificates. There was no way that mine was going anywhere and it is still tucked away among the memorabilia!

Many felt strongly as regards to the current owners' takeover, walking away from the club and never to return. If it is a history of the club that you are putting together, then a couple of trivia items from around the time of the takeover might be worth including in the collection.

When it comes to the history of Manchester United, the word 'Munich' casts a dark shadow over the club. But the disaster failed to register in my young mind and how I eventually discovered the horrors of that Thursday afternoon in Germany, I have no idea. Like many, however, it was to hold a strong fascination in later years and form a huge part of my United collection.

Glazer items.

The newspapers of the time are highly collectable, in particular the local Manchester editions from the day of the crash, with both the *Evening News* and the *Evening Chronicle* producing 'stop press' editions. The *Evening Chronicle* in its 'last extra' edition of 6 February carried the story that the United plane was held up in Germany and that Duncan Edwards should be fit for the Wolves match a couple of days later, while Kenny Morgans was doubtful. Their 'late night final', however, reported the grim news: 'United Air Disaster – 28 Killed'.

Speculation was rife, but the following morning it was front page news on all the national, and indeed international, titles, so there are countless newspapers to either collect or choose from to add to the collection. Remember too that every city, like Manchester, had its own newspaper(s), adding numerous more titles to the endless list of collectables. There are also numerous publications from overseas that covered the disaster.

Some of the programmes from around this time have already been included on previous pages, as have other items relating to some of the players who lost their lives, but there are other programmes out there to collect, with many clubs containing a reference to the disaster in their first home issue following the crash.

But what else is out there? A must-have item is the *Supporters Club Memorial Handbook*, which was produced after the crash. The word 'Keep' is prominent on the cover and I suspect that many have been and passed down over the years. This consists of some sixty-two pages, photographs of the players and journalists who lost their lives, as well as those who survived, along with photographs of the 1958 FA Cup Final and numerous articles.

Following the crash there were numerous memorial services and there are order of service sheets available for many.

The *Evening Despatch* following the Munich disaster.

SHREWSBURY TOWN
FOOTBALL CLUB LTD.

GAY MEADOW
PHONE 6068

OFFICIAL
PROGRAMME

6d.

FLOREAT SALOPIA

No. 32   Kick off 3-15 p.m.   SATURDAY, MARCH 15th, 1958

SPECIAL SOUVENIR PROGRAMME
Manchester United Disaster Fund

Our Club appeal to you good spectators of football to give this appeal your utmost support. All Clubs in the country have entered into the spirit of this appeal and our Club feel that this novel idea of contribution will give you all a chance of showing your generosity. The Joint Committee set up to deal with the Fund has outlined its plans as follows : — (1) Make Grants in cases of dire need to those who suffered physical or pecuniary loss, either in or as a consequence of the disaster and to their dependants. (2) Establish, if thought fit, suitable memorials to commemorate the Disaster.

The name by which the fund is known is, of course, "The Lord Mayor of Manchester's Munich Air Disaster Fund". Those who may benefit are not only the Manchester United personnel, which is the popular belief but also the relatives of Journalists, plus other civil personnel who were on the fated aircraft.

We quote from the F.A. News, 6th February, 1958 :—   **4300**

"**United in Life, United in Death.**"
In Memory of Roger Byrne, Captain and England left-back. Duncan Edwards, England left-half. Eddie Colman, David Pegg, Geoff Bent, Tommy Taylor, England centre-forward, Mark Jones, Bill Whelan, Eire inside-forward. Walter Crickmer, Secretary. Bert Whalley, coach, and Tom Curry, trainer.

Journalists : Henry Rose, Don Davies, Archie Ledbrooke, George Follows, Eric Thompson, Tom Jackson, Alf Clarke, Frank Swift, B. P. Miklos, W. T. Cable, W. Satinoff.

Our very good friend of the Supporters' Club and of so many Charities, Mrs. Wiggington is holding a Whist Drive on Monday next at the Morris Hall, at 7-30 p.m. *Note—***Monday, March 17th.** It is hoped that our Manager will be present to give the prizes and will be accompanied by some players. The proceeds of this Drive will be donated to the Disaster Fund.

BALL.
Our Ball today is given by the kindness of the Directors of **Rudge Roberts, Ltd., Wholesale Chemists,** and we convey our grateful thanks to that firm for their generous action.

Shrewsbury Town programme.

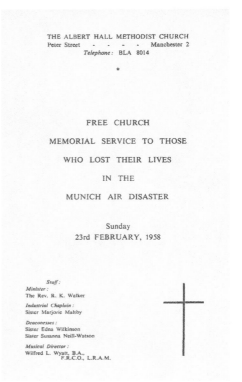

Above left: The *Supporters Club Memorial Handbook*, 1958.

Above right: Service sheet from one of the memorial services held after the Munich disaster.

More newspapers for the collection materialised some fifteen days after the crash, following the death of Duncan Edwards, the news once again casting a black cloud over Manchester and English football.

While mentioning Duncan Edwards, *Charles Buchan's Football Monthly* again comes to the fore, with the issue for March 1958 having a photograph of the player on its cover. As the magazine was published a month in advance, there was no mention of the disaster inside, but a small insert was included expressing their deepest sympathy to the club.

Auctions, appearing quite regularly these days, often conjure up items that belonged to an individual player, either being sold by the player in question or by someone who had it given to them by the player or someone related to the player. Personally I haven't bought at an auction, but there is the odd item within the collection that did belong to a United player.

First up is one of the gems in the collection – a Welsh international cap that belonged to the legendary Billy Meredith, said to be the first footballing superstar.

A dealer friend of mine had the cap, along with a signed photograph of the player, and upon a visit to his home he showed it to me and asked me if I was interested in it. At the time I was going through my non-pre-war phase and said thanks but no thanks and left without it. A while later I asked him if he still had it and he said yes, so I had a change of mind and procured it for the collection.

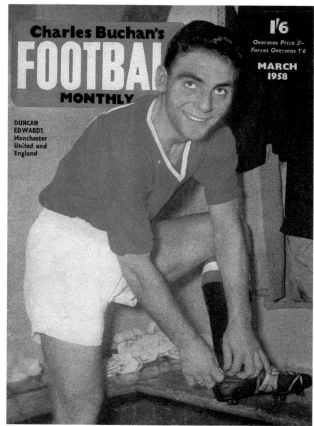

Above: The *Daily Mirror*, informing of Duncan Edwards' death.

Right: *Charles Buchan's Football Monthly* Edwards cover issue.

Billy Meredith's cap.

It was at the same time that my friend showed me another item that he had recently come across – a plaque from the 1952 FA Charity Shield match between United and Newcastle United that had belonged to full-back Tom McNulty. This did fall into my collecting area and I gladly took this off his hands. Before continuing, the programme for that FA Charity shield fixture against Newcastle is one of the hardest post-war United homes to obtain.

Another player-owned item I have is Paul McGrath's club blazer. This, funnily enough, was also obtained in a roundabout way. I had mentioned to a Manchester-based collecting friend that I would like to get a club blazer. Why, I do not know; perhaps just because they looked good. One night the telephone rang and my friend asked if I still fancied a club blazer, as there had been one advertised for sale in the *Manchester Evening News* the previous day, and he gave me the number of the seller.

Thinking that it would have been sold quickly, I left it, but decided a day later to ring the number. I asked if it was still available and was surprised when the woman on the other end of the phone said yes. I then asked whose it was and she replied Paul McGrath and that her husband had got it, adding that they now wanted to sell it and put the money towards a holiday. That's it, I thought, she wants quite a bit for it. I had no real idea what to offer, as she gave no other clue as to what she was looking for. In the end I think I said £75. She replied ok, and that was that.

Other personal items are player passes, with the one here having been owned by Colin Webster. These have the club rules and regulations included, which are interesting in their own right.

Right: Tom McNulty's plaque.

Below: Colin Webster's player pass.

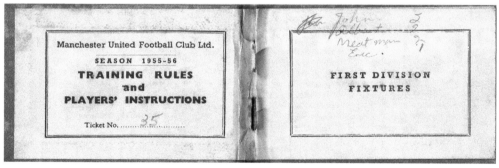

I also have a handful of telegrams sent to Stan Pearson, one of the star United players of that immediate post-war era. They were sent to Stan upon his selection for his first England international cap in April 1948 and prior to the 1948 FA Cup Final the following month. These are one-off items, which add a little special something to any collection.

Another player-owned item that has a tendency to turn up with some regularity is an away match itinerary, which were issued for European trips and Cup Finals. Small and pocket sized, some softback, some hard, they told the player where they had to be, or would be, at a given time during the trip.

With Manchester United having been formed by railway workers at the Newton Heath Carriage & Wagon Works, railway-related items can also find their way into the collection through leaflets promoting day trips to away games on a Football Special, or the tickets themselves. The latter may have little appeal to many, but they do form

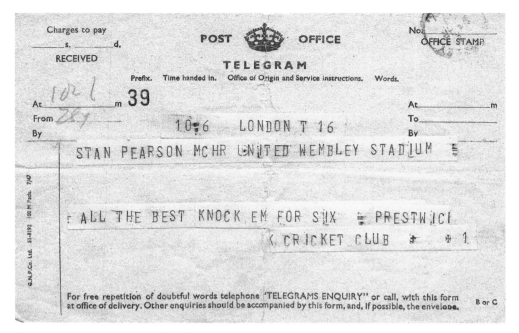

Two telegrams that were sent to Stan Pearson.

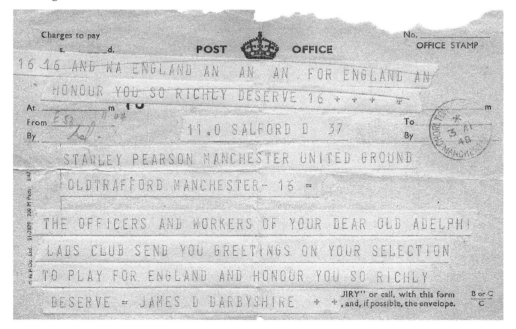

part of a travelling supporter's love affair with the club, with each individual ticket conjuring up a memory of a day out with the infamous Red Army.

Much of what has been written about so far has dwelt in a bygone age, a golden age of football and certainly of collecting, but what of modern-day items?

Above: Player itinerary.

Right: A railway flier.

SATURDAY 7TH FEBRUARY 1987
TODAY LEAGUE DIVISION 1
CHARLTON ATHLETIC
v
MANCHESTER UNITED
AT SELHURST PARK   KO 15.00
OUTWARDS   RETURN
10.36   Manchester Piccadilly 20.14
10.44   Stockport   20.06
14.20   Norwood Junction   17.08

2ND CLASS RETURN FARE £10.00
NO HALF FARES

ACCOMMODATION LIMITED
BOOK IN ADVANCE

Passengers will be issued with
special tickets which are only
valid for travel by this service.

The Board do not undertake to
refund fares in the event of
cancellations of this match.
No alcohol allowed on this service.
Light refreshments available.
All fares and facilities shown are
subject to alteration or
cancellation

Corinthian ProStar figures proved immensely popular when they first hit the marketplace, but have since been confined to near obscurity, as have their various rivals, although if they have been kept intact in the original packaging, some might still have a value out there.

However, it was another form of figurine, much more attractive in appearance compared to the Corinthians, that became an instant collectable – the Corgi Icon, which appeared during the 1998/99 season. These were originally priced at £14.99 and issued with a certificate stating that it was part of a United set of 1,000. Those figures appeared in both the red home shirt and the blue away shirt of the time.

A Corgi Icon figure.

Match day badges, displaying the crests of the two opposing clubs, appear to be popular, but whether they have any long-lasting value remains to be seen. But one match day item that will prove to be worthless, while also being despised by not just the serious collector but also the long-standing supporter, is the dreaded half-and-half scarf, of which no more will be said.

It is the items of the past that continue to be sought after; those obscure bits and pieces that turn up out of the blue. Items such as those illustrated alongside: a car park pass for the Old Trafford forecourt from the mid-1950s and a press pass or a card that was sent out by the club thanking members of the public for their good wishes upon winning the First Division title in 1957.

What about cloth patches, of which there are many? Or handwritten team sheets from the dressing room? The latter might not grasp the imagination, but I should add that the handwritten team sheet for Sir Alex Ferguson's first game in charge at Oxford in November 1986 sold for a remarkable £19,000 at auction. Given to the seller as a gift, it was expected to fetch £3,000, which in itself was quite a price for what it was.

BBC Wiltshire got in touch with me and asked what I thought about the item and the expected price, and I certainly did not expect anything like £19,000. Not wanting to be quoted on a figure, I simply said that it really depended on who was at the auction on the day and how much they wanted it, and that it could go for less than the estimate or a bit more.

Press photographs are also something to consider, and are something that can provide a different side to building a photographic club history. Many of those that are out there and available have never been previously published and can be little more than random shots, taken at the time, developed and simply left to gather dust on shelves or in filing cabinets.

FOOTBALL MATCHES AT OLD TRAFFORD

Traffic Regulations—PERMIT

SEASON 1953-54

Allow Bearer with Car

to proceed to Manchester United Football Ground
and park in front of the offices.

Permit issued on the understanding that Car reaches ground 15 minutes before Kick-off and does not leave until after crowd has left and congestion on roads has eased.

J Waddington

CHIEF SUPERINTENDENT,
LANCASHIRE CONSTABULARY,
Divisional Headquarters, Old Trafford

A car park pass.

May, 1957

The Chairman and Directors
wish to acknowledge with grateful thanks
your kind message of congratulation on the team's
success in winning the League Championship
The host of communications is significant
that we are in the thoughts of our countless friends
and has created added warmth
to the happy atmosphere which abounds the Club
in it's hour of triumph.

Old Trafford,
Manchester 16.

Above: The card sent out by the club after winning the league in 1957.

Left: A Manchester United Supporters Club patch.

The variety of what is out there is vast, with everything from player portraits to team groups or some opportune shot captured for posterity. Three good examples shown here all come from the Arsenal match in February 1958, the Busby Babes' last match in England prior to Munich. They are all postcard size and, as you can see, they are not in the best of condition, but this is something that would for once not deter the collector.

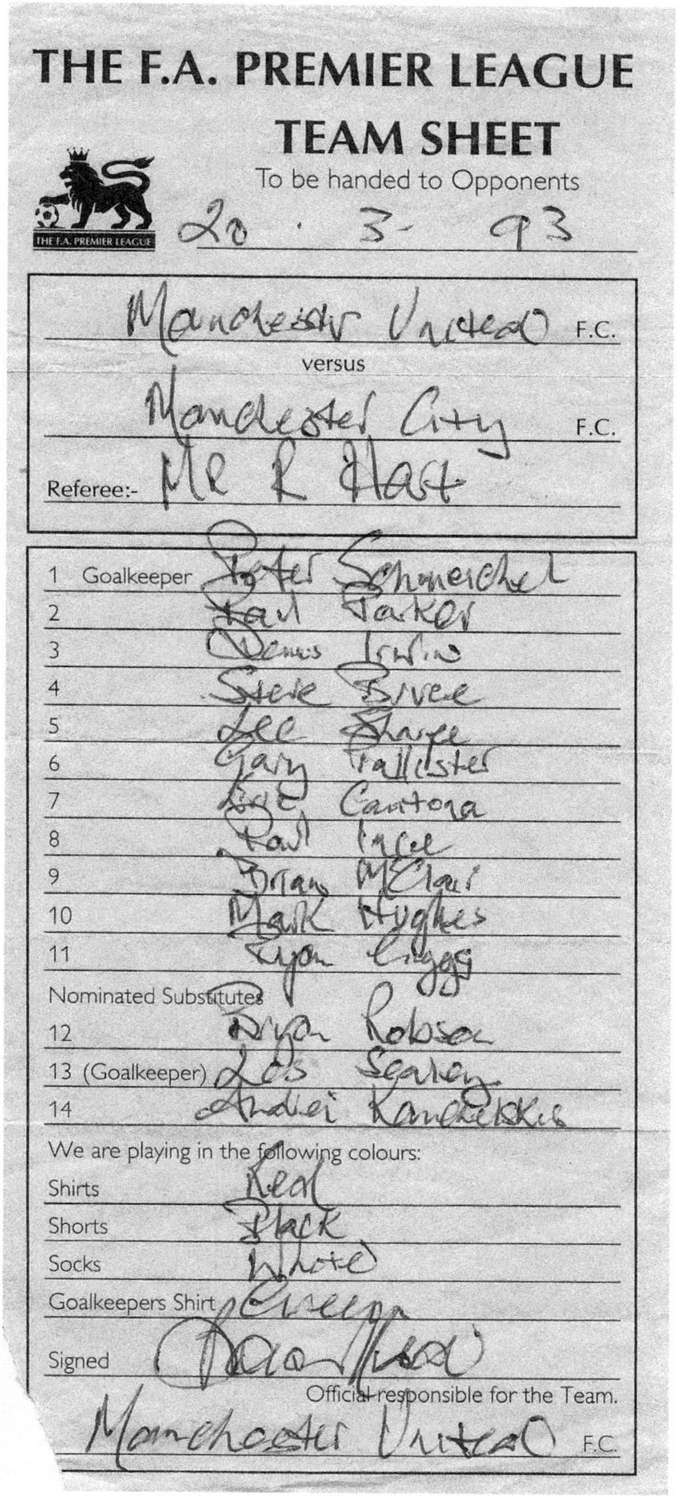

THE F.A. PREMIER LEAGUE
TEAM SHEET
To be handed to Opponents

20 . 3 - 93

Manchester United F.C.

versus

Manchester City F.C.

Referee:- Mr R Hart

1	Goalkeeper	Peter Schmeichel
2		Paul Parker
3		Denis Irwin
4		Steve Bruce
5		Lee Sharpe
6		Gary Pallister
7		Eric Cantona
8		Paul Ince
9		Brian McClair
10		Mark Hughes
11		Ryan Giggs

Nominated Substitutes

12		Bryan Robson
13	(Goalkeeper)	Les Sealey
14		Andrei Kanchelskis

We are playing in the following colours:

Shirts — Red
Shorts — Black
Socks — White
Goalkeepers Shirt — Green

Signed (Alex Ferguson)

Official responsible for the Team.

Manchester United F.C.

Handwritten team sheet.

Roger Byrne leads out the team for their last match on English soil, at Highbury in February 1958, prior to the Munich disaster.

Action from the match against Arsenal at Highbury in February 1958.

Duncan Edwards signs an autograph prior to the match against Arsenal at Highbury in February 1958.

How about records? I bought a recording of the 1968 European Cup Final, with highlights of the first and second half on one side and extra time on the flip if I remember rightly. How about 'Onward Sexton's Soldiers'? I didn't buy that one and have no idea where it materialised from, but it is in there with everything else.

Another record I have, although this one is in a frame and is up in the loft, is the 'United Calypso' by Edric Connor, which was released in 1957. This is one of those old 78 rpm discs, and it may not have ever been played. I recently heard of one selling for

EC Cup Final record.

£50! Also in the frame is the sheet music, which in itself is a lovely item to have and would certainly look good in a frame on its own. This could well cost you more than the record, and it is better to look at.

There is a saying that a dog is not just for Christmas, which I now intend to re-word into saying that a Christmas card is not just for Christmas, as they make an appearance in many collections. Each year the United staff and management send out countless cards, some eye catching and instantly collectable, others, although being tucked away for posterity, are only added to the collection through force of habit. The one illustrated from 1960 shows a view of the ground that many who attend games today would fail to recognise as Old Trafford. It was also sent to someone by Jimmy Murphy.

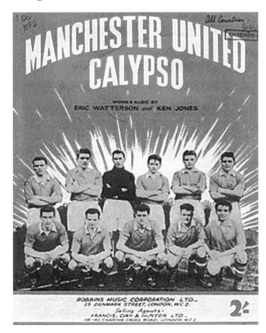

Sheet music for the 'United Calypso'.

A Christmas card from 1960.

M.U.F.C.

———

DINNER

13TH OCTOBER, 1960

———

Please present this
portion on entering
the Derby Suite

Manchester United
v.
Real Madrid

The Directors of
Manchester United Football Club Ltd.

request the pleasure of the company of

D. Gaskell, Esq., and Lady

at Dinner
in the Midland Hotel, Manchester
on Thursday, 13th October, 1960 at 10 p.m. for 10-15 p.m.

No acknowledgment required   *Ordinary Dress*

A Manchester United *v.* Real Madrid invitation.

Everyone likes an invite and again there is quite a variety out there from various banquets, etc. given by the club, The one featured here was sent to David Gaskell, requesting his presence at an after-match dinner following a friendly against Real Madrid in 1960.

Space is beginning to run out, so what have I not covered that I can squeeze in? Pennants, for one. This is another item that is more a relic from days gone by, with small plastic ones produced during that 1968 European Cup run, and another produced for the League Championship success in 1965. The odd modern-day ones do materialise, however, and also shown is one produced by Feyenoord for the Europa League Tie in September 2016.

Car stickers will seldom be kept, but one for the 1967 Championship win has survived the test of time, with another in a scrapbook of match reports.

Souvenir pennant for the 1968 European Cup Final against Benfica.

A Championship pennant.

A Feyenoord pennant.

A Manchester United car sticker, 1967.

Chapter 8

The Ones That Got Away

Adding items to the collection today is infrequent to say the least, but odds and ends do still find their way into the filing cabinet and cupboards to join all the other odds and ends already accumulated; bits and pieces from the club pre-season tours, for instance, thanks to friends.

Almost anything is welcomed, but what of the items that have escaped my grasp, the ones that have got away or, more to the point, that I have allowed to pass me by; the regrets, of which two instantly spring to mind.

The first comes from what must have been the late 1970s when I received a list, which I still have to this day, from Ian Peters of Goal-Line Clearance Programmes in Stourbridge, the West Midlands. It wasn't a programme list, my main collecting thing at that time, but one covering copies of the *Sporting Chronicle* newspaper from the 1880s.

2018 tour item.

This fifteen-page list contained copies of the *Chronicle* from 1 January 1889 up until December 1892, detailing the clubs featured in each issue, with the price for each issue alongside. This, by the way, was not an auction, and was rather first come first serve.

I didn't buy any. Why not, I have no idea; probably because I was not really into pre-war items at the time and, as previously mentioned, I preferred programmes. Perhaps the prices might have put me off a little, but I honestly do not know. However, I do know that I regret it very much now, as match reports and cuttings are now very much 'my thing'.

So, let's turn the pages of this fascinating list, even today, and see what I didn't buy.

The pages begin with Ian Peters writing: 'Now when you consider that very few programmes were printed before 1900, then you begin to realize that these are not just newspapers but probably the oldest record, if not the only item you will ever be able to collect from the very early days of football.'

The first Newton Heath report was in that very first paper, dated 1 January 1889, and covered a friendly against Third Lanark. This copy was described as substandard and was priced at £9. All the prices, by the way, included recorded delivery postage in a waterproof plastic bag. Numerous issues followed and were generally priced at £12, although one, dated 29 April 1889 and covering the Manchester Senior Cup Final against Hooley Hill, was £22.

Over the fifteen pages, you can imagine that there is a fair bit of Newton Heath content and to have bought everything would have come to a few pounds. However, the ones that I do regret not investing in were as follows: 2 January 1892, a report on the Newton Heath AGM; 13 April 1892, which covered a meeting that would turn the club into a limited company and cost £15; 29 April 1892, a large article covering the court case of a printer against Newton Heath over alleged debts by a previous secretary; 6 May 1892, more on the limited company business; 12 May 1892, more on the club becoming a limited company, as well as future plans for the club covered in detail; and 15 July 1892, a report on securing North Road for the coming season. They were all priced at between £9 and £12, while an issue from 16 October 1892, which covered the record-breaking 10-1 game against Wolves, was £24.

Why have I kept the list? Originally, as it gave dates of reports, with no statistical books back then – I also collated such things in those days – they were worth keeping hold of.

Just going back to the papers for a minute, perhaps even more valuable today than any of the Newton Heath issues are those from January and March 1892, which dealt with meetings of Everton FC that led to the formation of Liverpool. What would such items be priced at today?

I mentioned two regrets. The second was maybe twenty odd years ago, when I visited a card fair in Blackpool and one seller had an enormous amount of cigarette/trade cards. I didn't bother with those pre-war cards, but regret now not buying the United ones on sale. I probably have them all, or at least most of them, now, but I still regret not buying them back then.

So, full time beckons, and we have taken a whirlwind adventure through the world of Manchester United collectables.

A whole book could have been filled with United programmes from home and abroad, and another with match tickets from countless venues, again in Britain and in countries from America to Australia and back again. Cards in the various shapes and forms would fill another volume.

But I had to make a choice and select from the vast array of items at my disposal, and I hope that those that I have chosen fit their purpose, giving this book a dash of colour, a little style and, above all, capture your imagination and make you want to seek out some of those items that are illustrated. That is, if you don't already have them all already.

If you do, then you will perhaps be bidding against me for other items to add to the collection, as well as searching the various listing and catalogues for those illusive pieces of memorabilia from yesteryear.

Remember that collecting is mainly for enjoyment and what you collect is entirely down to your own personal choice. Mine? Match reports and newspaper cuttings.

Hopefully you have found this book of interest. I have enjoyed compiling it, as I have enjoyed collecting Manchester United memorabilia over the years. It has certainly come a long way since that Jackie Blanchflower Chix card and that programme against Burnley.